CAMPAIGN 364

# THE NETHERLANDS EAST INDIES CAMPAIGN 1941–42

Japan's Quest for Oil

**MARC LOHNSTEIN**  ILLUSTRATED BY GRAHAM TURNER
*Series editor Nikolai Bogdanovic*

OSPREY PUBLISHING
Bloomsbury Publishing Plc
Kemp House, Chawley Park, Cumnor Hill, Oxford OX2 9PH, UK
29 Earlsfort Terrace, Dublin 2, Ireland
1385 Broadway, 5th Floor, New York, NY 10018, USA
E-mail: info@ospreypublishing.com
www.ospreypublishing.com

OSPREY is a trademark of Osprey Publishing Ltd

First published in Great Britain in 2021

© Osprey Publishing Ltd, 2021

All rights reserved. No part of this publication may be reproduced or transmitted in any form or by any means, electronic or mechanical, including photocopying, recording, or any information storage or retrieval system, without prior permission in writing from the publishers.

A catalogue record for this book is available from the British Library.

ISBN: PB 9781472843524; eBook 9781472843531; ePDF 9781472843548; XML 9781472843555

21 22 23 24 25   10 9 8 7 6 5 4 3 2 1

Maps by Bounford.com
3D BEVs by Paul Kime
Index by Angela Hall
Typeset by PDQ Digital Media Solutions, Bungay, UK
Printed and bound in India by Replika Press Private Ltd.

## Artist's note

Readers may care to note that the original paintings from which the colour plates in this book were prepared are available for private sale. All reproduction copyright whatsoever is retained by the publishers. All enquiries should be addressed to:
Graham Turner, PO Box 568, Aylesbury, Bucks, HP17 8ZX, UK
www.studio88.co.uk
The publishers regret that they can enter into no correspondence upon this matter.

Osprey Publishing supports the Woodland Trust, the UK's leading woodland conservation charity.

To find out more about our authors and books visit www.ospreypublishing.com. Here you will find extracts, author interviews, details of forthcoming events and the option to sign up for our newsletter.

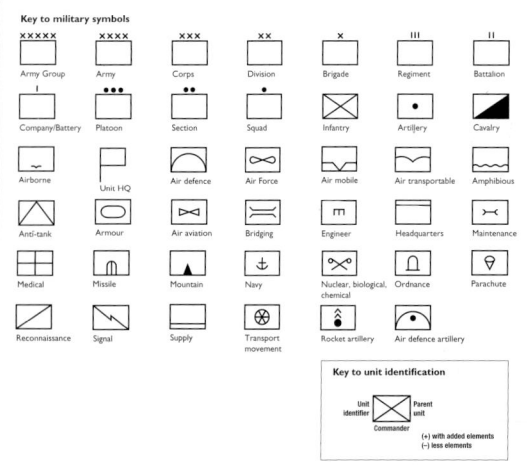

## Author's acknowledgements

For his valuable comments on my text I would like to thank Mark Loderichs. Thanks also to Ishida Noriko for helping to select and acquire photos from Japan. I am also indebted to the staff of the Netherlands Institute of Military History, NIOD, NMvW and Mariniersmuseum; the owners of private collections who provided photographs for this volume; and my editor Nikolai Bogdanovic.

## Colonial vs modern place names

| Colonial name | Modern Indonesian name |
|---|---|
| Atamboea | Atambua |
| Atjeh | Aceh |
| Bandoeng | Bandung |
| Bandjermasin | Banjarmasin |
| Bantam | Banten |
| Batavia | Jakarta |
| Benkoelen | Bengkulu |
| Billiton | Belitung |
| Boeroe | Buru |
| Buitenzorg | Bogor |
| Celebes | Sulawesi |
| Cheribon | Cirebon |
| Djambi | Jambi |
| Djatisari | Jatisari |
| Djokjakarta | Yogyakarta |
| Hitoe | Hitu |
| Indramajoe | Indramayu |
| Kalidjati | Kalijati |
| Koepang | Kupang |
| Koetaradja | Banda Aceh |
| Madioen | Madiun |
| Madoera | Madura |
| Martapoera | Martapura |
| Menado | Manado |
| Moentok | Muntok |
| Moesi | Musi |
| Oosthaven | Bandar Lampung |
| Pakan-Baroe | Pakan-Baru |
| Pamanoekan | Pamanukan |
| Penfoei | Penfui |
| Pladjoe | Plaju |
| Poerwakarta | Purwakarta |
| Praboemoelih | Prabumulih |
| Preanger | Parahyangan or Priangan |
| Rangkasbitoeng | Rangkasbitung |
| Riouw | Riau |
| Soengei Gerong | Sungei Gerong |
| Serajoe Rivier | Serayu River |
| Soebang | Subang |
| Soerabaja | Surabaya |
| Soerakarta | Surakarta (Solo) |
| Talangbetoetoe | Talangbetutu |
| Tandjong Priok | Tanjung Priok |
| Tjepoe | Cepu |
| Tjianten rivier | Cianten River |
| Tjiater | Ciater |
| Tjilatjap | Cilacap |
| Tjioedjoeng Rivier | Ciujung River |
| Tjitaroem Rivier | Citarum River |
| Toeban | Tuban |
| Waigapoe | Waingapu |

## A note on time

In this work, times are given as offsets (hours/minutes) from Coordinated Universal Time (UTC). The Netherlands East Indies had several time zones. The below list is provided to help readers:
CBT    Celebes Time (observed in Sulawesi and on Timor) UTC+08:00
CSST   Central and Southern Sumatra Time (observed in Bengkulu, Palembang and Lampung) UTC+07:00
JST    Japan Standard Time (a.k.a. Tokyo Time) UTC+09:00
JBBT   Java Time (observed on Java, Bali and Borneo) UTC+07:30
MCT    Moluccan Time (observed in Ternate, Namlea, Ambon and Banda) UTC+08:30
NST    Northern Sumatra Time (observed in Tapanuli and Aceh) UTC+06:30

**PREVIOUS PAGE**
Japanese troops at Palembang. (Mainichi Newspapers)

# CONTENTS

## ORIGINS OF THE CAMPAIGN 5
Japanese expansion . Oil: fuel for ships, planes and war . Moving south

## CHRONOLOGY 8

## OPPOSING COMMANDERS 10
Japanese . Allied

## OPPOSING FORCES 16
Japanese . RNEI Army . Allies . Orders of battle

## OPPOSING PLANS 27
Japanese . Netherlands East Indies . Allies

## THE CAMPAIGN 37
Phase I operations . Phase II operations: the conquest of the NEI . Tarakan . Menado . Balikpapan Kendari . Singkawang . Ambon . Makassar . Bandjermasin . Palembang (Operation *L*) . Bali Timor . Java (Operation *H*) . Surrender . Operation *T* (northern Sumatra)

## AFTERMATH 91

## FURTHER READING 94

## INDEX 95

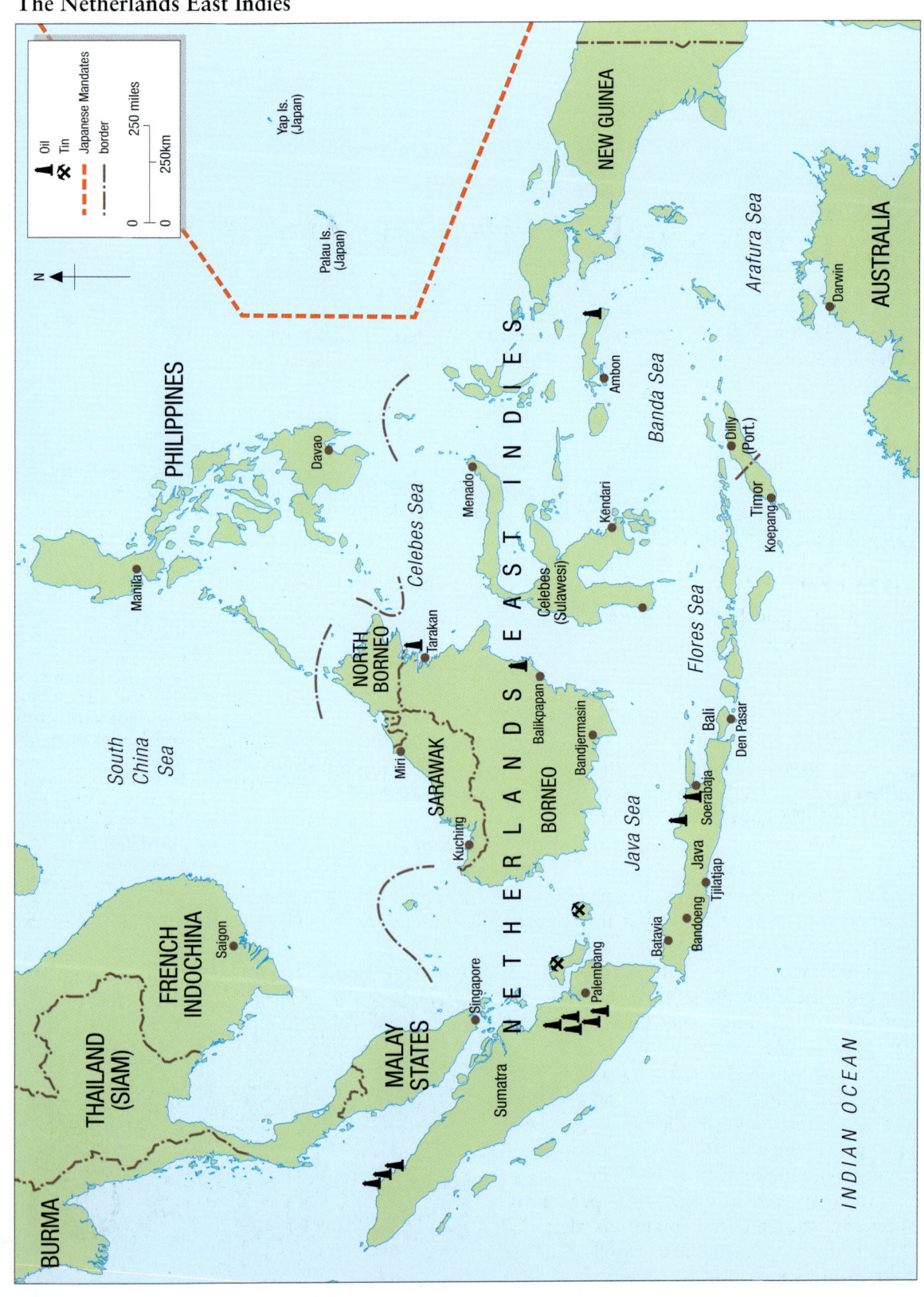

# ORIGINS OF THE CAMPAIGN

In December 1941, Japan took up arms against the Western Powers in what it claimed to be a struggle of self-defence and self-preservation. In just a few months, Japan subdued South-East Asia and created a Greater East Asian Co-Prosperity Sphere. It took the Allies nearly four years to defeat Japan and retake the area.

The Japanese Southern Offensive, Operation *A-Go*, consisted of three major campaigns: Malaya, the Philippines and the Netherlands East Indies. This work describes the attack on and conquest of the Netherlands East Indies. Among the questions it will seek to answer are: What place did the Netherlands East Indies (NEI, present-day Indonesia) occupy in the Japanese war goals? How did Japan intend to achieve this? What were the defensive plans of the Netherlands East Indies? And how did the campaign progress at the operational and tactical level?

## JAPANESE EXPANSION

Japan's expansion into China brought it into conflict with the other major powers in Asia. Border fighting even took place with the Soviet Union in 1938 and 1939. Great Britain could do little to counter this expansion. Even prior to World War I, it lacked the means to simultaneously maintain battle fleets in European and Asian waters. It was the United States that took the lead in curbing Japan's drive to expand. The US wished not only to halt the Japanese expansion of power, but also to curb it. To this end, it imposed ever more stringent economic sanctions and military pressure by moving, in 1940, most of the US fleet from the US Pacific coast to Hawaii, and stationing B-17 long-range bombers in the Philippines. The sanctions would be lifted if Japan withdrew from China and French Indochina. Japan thus would not only have to give up its empire and aspirations to become a great power, but also would have to submit to the economic supremacy of the United States.

Japan looked at ways of peacefully accessing strategic raw materials that the US was denying it, and its gaze fell upon the Netherlands East Indies.

In this 1930s aerial photo, the Bataafsche Petroleum Maatschappij (BPM) oil refineries at Plaju can be seen in the centre foreground (with the residential area to the right), while in the left background are the refineries of the Nederlandsche Koninklijke Petroleum Maatschappij (NKPM) at Sungai Gerong, east of Palembang, South Sumatra. To the left is the Musi River. The refineries jointly accounted for one-third of total NEI oil production. This was the only source of high-quality aviation fuel (100 octane) in the NEI. The main oil wells were at Djambi. NKPM was a subsidiary of the American Standard Oil Company. BPM was owned by Royal Dutch Shell. (Leiden University Libraries, KITLV 2790)

# OIL: FUEL FOR SHIPS, PLANES AND WAR

Oil was the Achilles' heel of the Japanese Empire. It depended almost entirely on imports for its consumption, as shown in Table 1. The United States supplied more than half of Japan's oil consumption, and thus an American oil embargo would hit Japan hard. The Netherlands East Indies provided a logical, if not sole, alternative to American oil, one that could meet Japan's needs.

**Table 1: Japanese oil supply 1937–39 (million barrels)**

| Year | Consumption | Own production | Import | United States | Netherlands East Indies | Other |
|---|---|---|---|---|---|---|
| 1937 | 41 | 3.1 | 38 | 25 | 10 | 3 |
| 1938 | 46 | 3.0 | 43 | 30 | 10 | 3 |
| 1939 | 40 | 3.1 | 36.8 | 19.4 | 14.1 | 3.3 |

In addition to oil, the Netherlands East Indies was also an important source of natural rubber, tin and bauxite. In 1938, worldwide demand for natural rubber was 933,000 tons: the Netherlands East Indies accounted for 302,872 tons, or 32 per cent of the world market. In 1938, 27,737 kilotonnes of tin was extracted there out of the *c.* 148,100 long tons worldwide, in third place after Malaya and Bolivia. The Netherlands East Indies also quarried 245,354 tons of bauxite in 1938. It also produced 90 per cent of the cinchona plant, and thus had a monopoly on the main anti-malarial drug: quinine.

**Table 2: The Netherlands East Indies oil industry (million barrels)**

| Year | Production (including British Borneo) | Netherlands East Indies consumption | Export (excluding Japan) | Export to Japan |
|---|---|---|---|---|
| 1937 | 59.8 | 18.4 | 31.4 | 10 |
| 1938 | 61.3 | 19.7 | 31.5 | 10 |
| 1939 | 66.0 | 19.8 | 32.1 | 14.1 |

Given the importance of the Netherlands East Indies as a supplier of strategic raw materials, Japan was committed to bringing the area within its sphere of influence: the Greater East Asian Co-Prosperity Sphere. Between 1940 and 1941, Japan began negotiations to increase its influence in the Netherlands East Indies and to acquire the necessary strategic raw materials by peaceful means. However, Japan complicated these negotiations by establishing an alliance with Germany and Italy in September 1940: the Tripartite Pact. The Netherlands had been at war with and subsequently occupied by Germany since May that year. The Japanese threat was clearly felt. The Netherlands East Indies took part in military staff conferences with Great Britain and Australia in Singapore to coordinate joint actions in the event of war with Japan. The United States was present as an observer. The Netherlands felt strengthened by these staff conferences with regard to Japan. However, concrete political commitments were not forthcoming from Great Britain and the United States. The Netherlands East Indies delayed negotiations with Japan. It was also unwilling to join the Greater East Asian Co-Prosperity Sphere. The talks did not bring Japan the result it had expected, and they were therefore ended in June 1941.

# MOVING SOUTH

The Japanese occupation of the southern Chinese island of Hainan in 1939 and the deployment of troops in northern French Indochina in 1940 and southern French Indochina in July 1941 brought the British possessions of Malaya and Singapore, and the Netherlands East Indies, within reach of Japanese land-based aircraft. It also put further pressure on the Netherlands to meet the Japanese requirements. However, this move southwards sparked a fierce response from the United States. It froze Japanese assets on 26 July 1941. A total shutdown of oil supplies was not intended, but in fact the American response boiled down to that. Great Britain agreed to it, and the Netherlands reluctantly followed, aware that taking part in the embargo meant war with Japan.

Japan was faced with the feared oil embargo, and its attempt to peacefully create an alternative in the form of increased supplies from the Netherlands East Indies had also failed. For Japan, in light of the US economic stranglehold, only two choices remained open: to yield to US demands, or to acquire the necessary raw materials by force. Japan chose the latter. The American policy to keep Japan from further expansion in South-East Asia through economic and military pressure had failed.

For Japan to have a chance to win a military conflict at all, it would need to act in 1940–41. The war in Europe had severely weakened its potential opponents and/or tied down their forces elsewhere. The balance of power had shifted in favour of Japan. With the Two-Ocean Navy Act of July 1940, the US had initiated a major naval construction programme. Japan saw a window of opportunity. It was now or never.

Tarakan is a small, hilly and jungle-covered island off the east coast of Borneo. The crude oil that was extracted from the island was sold directly as fuel without refining. Tarakan accounted for 9 per cent of total NEI petroleum production. The island had two drilling sites and an oil tank farm for storage. The image shows derricks probably at Pamusian c. 1940. (Leiden University Libraries, KITLV 176800)

# CHRONOLOGY

## 1941

| | |
|---|---|
| 1 December | Military Aviation Service of the Royal Netherlands East Indies (RNEI) Army (*Wapen der Militaire Luchtvaart van het Koninklijk Nederlands-Indisch Leger*, ML-KNIL) is mobilized. |
| 7/8 December | Japanese attacks on Pearl Harbor, Malaya, Hong Kong and the Philippines. |
| 8 December | The Netherlands declares war on Japan. |
| | Partial NEI mobilization in outlying areas, and of coastal, anti-aircraft artillery and searchlight personnel, on Java, Madura, Bali and Lombok. |
| 9 December | NEI troops turn out for the partial mobilization. |
| | Aircraft Group (*Vliegtuiggroep*, Vl.G.) and a fighter squadron of the RNEI Army Military Aviation Service are stationed in Singapore. |
| 10 December | Destruction of British naval Force Z: HMS *Prince of Wales* and HMS *Repulse* are sunk by Japanese aircraft. |
| 11 December | General mobilization of the RNEI Army. |
| 12 December | NEI troops turn out for the general mobilization. |
| | Sparrow Force disembarks on Timor. |
| 16 December | Japanese landing and capture of Miri, British Borneo. |
| 17 December | Gull Force disembarks on Ambon. |
| | Netherlands–Australian expedition disembarks at Dilly, Portuguese Timor. |
| 24 December | Japanese landing at Kuching, British Borneo. |
| 27 December | Japanese forces occupy the NEI Tambelan Islands in the South China Sea. |
| 29 December | 19th Bombardment Group (USAAF) transfers from Australia to Malang, Java. |

## 1942

| | |
|---|---|
| 10 January | General A.P. Wavell and his staff arrive at Batavia (Jakarta). |
| 11 January | Japan declares war on the Netherlands. |
| | Japanese landings on Tarakan and at Menado. Menado is taken. |
| | HQ 26th Field Artillery Brigade and 2nd Battalion, 131st Field Artillery Regiment (both US Army) disembark at Surabaya, Java. |
| 12 January | RNEI Army garrison in Tarakan surrenders, formalized the following day. |
| 15 January | American-British-Dutch-Australian Command (ABDACOM) is activated. |
| 18 January | Transfer of HQ No. 225 (Bomber) Group (RAF) from Singapore to Palembang, Sumatra. |
| 24 January | Japanese amphibious landings at, and capture of, Balikpapan (East Borneo) and Kendari (Sulawesi). |
| | Naval engagement at Balikpapan. |
| 27 January | Japanese capture of Singkawang II Airfield (West Borneo). |
| 30 January | Japanese occupation of Pontianak, West Borneo. |
| 31 January | Japanese amphibious landings on Ambon and conquest of Ambon City. |
| 1 February | Main body of RNEI Army troops surrenders on Ambon. |
| | Formation of HQ No. 226 (Fighter) Group (RAF) in Palembang, Sumatra. |
| 2 February | Arrival of British 6th Heavy Anti-Aircraft Regiment (reduced) and 78th Battery, 35th Light Anti-Aircraft Regiment (RA) in Palembang. |
| 3 February | Surrender of Gull Force on Ambon. |

|  |  |
|---|---|
| 4/5 February | Naval action in the Makassar Strait. Japanese air attacks on the Combined Striking Force. |
| 4 February | British 77th Heavy Anti-Aircraft Regiment (RA), 21st and 48th Light Anti-Aircraft regiments (RA) and HQ 16th Anti-Aircraft Brigade disembark at Jakarta. |
| 7 February | Japanese occupation of Samarinda (East Borneo). |
| 9 February | Japanese amphibious landing at, and conquest of, Makassar. |
| 10 February | Japanese occupation of Bandjermasin. |
| 14 February | Japanese airborne landings at Palembang and capture of Palembang I Airfield. |
| | British B Squadron, 3rd The King's Own Hussars disembark in South Sumatra. |
| 15 February | Japanese landing on Bangka. |
| | Naval action in the Gaspar Strait. |
| | Japanese occupation of Palembang. |
| | The fall of Singapore. |
| | ABDACOM decides to evacuate South Sumatra. |
| 19 February | Japanese landing on and conquest of Bali. |
| | Japanese air raid on Darwin, northern Australia. |
| | Combined Chiefs of Staff decide not to send Australian I Corps to Java. |
| | Disembarkation at Jakarta of part of the Australian 7th Division advance guard and formation of 'Blackforce'. |
| 19/20 February | Naval Battle of Badung Strait (Bali). |
| 20 February | Japanese landings on Timor and conquest of Kupang and Dilly. |
| 22 February | Decision to withdraw United States Army Air Forces (USAAF) units from Java. |
| 23 February | Surrender of Sparrow Force on Dutch Timor. |
| | ABDACOM is dissolved. |
| 27 February | USS *Langley* (carrying a cargo of fighters) is sunk south of Java. |
| 27/28 February | Battle of the Java Sea. |
| 28 February /1 March | Japanese landings on Java. |
| | Naval action in Bantam Bay (Battle of Sunda Strait). |
| 1 March | Japanese Shoji Detachment takes Kalidjati Airfield. |
| | East Group (USAAF) begins evacuating from Java to Australia. |
| 2 March | Counter-attack by the RNEI Army Mobile Unit (*Mobiele Eenheid*) at Subang. |
| 3/5 March | Battle at Leuwiliang between units from the Japanese 2nd Division and Blackforce. |
| 3 March | Counter-attacks by 2nd Infantry Regiment (reinforced) and RNEI Army Teerink Group on Kalidjati fail due to air attacks. |
| 5 March | Japanese Shoji Detachment attacks the Ciater defensive position. |
| | Jakarta is evacuated by the RNEI Army and occupied by the Japanese. |
| 6 March | Ciater defensive position breached by the Japanese. |
| 7 March | RNEI Army Bandung Group offers local surrender. |
| 8 March | Negotiations concerning the RNEI Army's complete surrender take place in Kalidjati. |
| | Cilacap and Surabaya are occupied by the Japanese. |
| 9 March | The RNEI Army surrenders. |
| 12 March | Surrender of Allied armed forces in Java. |
| | Japanese Imperial Guard Division lands in North Sumatra. |
| 28 March | Surrender of RNEI Army troops in North and Central Sumatra. |

# OPPOSING COMMANDERS

## JAPANESE

**Lieutenant-General Hitoshi Imamura (1886–1968)** was the commander of the Sixteenth Army in 1942. He became an officer in 1907. Imamura had inside knowledge of the British Army: in 1917, he was posted to London for three years as Deputy Military Attaché, and in 1927 was an attaché in British India. In addition to these foreign postings, he gained staff experience with the Operations Section of the Imperial Japanese General Staff and with the staff of the Kwantung Army in Manchuria. He had operational experience in China as a regimental and division commander. From 1940 to June 1941, he served as the deputy chief of the influential Inspectorate General of Military Training. On 6 November 1941, his appointment by the emperor as commander of the Sixteenth Army followed, a prestigious assignment. The Netherlands East Indies was the final piece of the Southern Offensive. Due to the great distances and loss of its signal equipment, Imamura had limited command and control over the Sixteenth Army during the campaign in Java.

After the war, he was charged with war crimes by the Australian government. He was found guilty and sentenced to ten years' imprisonment. In 1948–49, the Temporary Courts-Martial in Jakarta also brought him to trial for war crimes in Borneo and Java. However, he was acquitted.

Imamura was known in the Japanese military for his 'bravery as a commander with a resolute and indomitable fighting spirit'. He was a skilled organizer and willing to take great operational risks. The landing of the Shoji Detachment was decidedly daring, but also bordered on the reckless.

**Colonel Toshishige Shoji (1890–1974)** was commander of the 230th Infantry Regiment, 38th Division in 1941. This regiment took part in the conquest of Hong Kong in December 1941 and the attack on Java in March 1942. Imamura personally chose Shoji to lead an important secondary operation in Java with a small regimental battle group. He trusted that Shoji would act

As commanding officer of the newly formed Sixteenth Army, the 55-year-old Hitoshi Imamura was tasked with conquering the Netherlands East Indies. A skilled organizer, his operational plan was extremely daring. When landing on Java, his ship was torpedoed by friendly fire; he was pitched into the oil-covered water, and rescued some hours later. (Mainichi Newspapers)

**FAR LEFT**
Colonel Toshishige Shoji was an old acquaintance of Imamura's. They had served together in various units for quite some time. On 2 March 1942, at Subang, Shoji was surprised by the counter-attack of the NEI Mobile Unit. The Dutch were unaware of the presence of his headquarters and drove on. In September 1942, the 230th Infantry Regiment, 38th Division was moved to Rabaul and deployed to Guadalcanal. There it suffered heavy casualties against American troops. The failure on Guadalcanal resulted in Shoji being transferred from a front-line unit to a depot and garrison unit. At the end of the war, he was the commanding officer of the Sendai Area Command, Japan. This photo was taken after his promotion to major-general in March 1944. (Public domain)

**LEFT**
Major-General Saburo Endo commanded the 3rd Air Division. This unit was involved in the Malaya, South Sumatra and the Java campaigns. He was an experienced staff officer. On 3 March 1942, he flew to Kalijdati. His aircraft smashed the major NEI counter-attack on the airfield. Endo then supported Shoji's attack against Ciater. On his own initiative, he shifted the focus from providing air support for the advance in West Java to the attack on Bandung. It was also Endo who, before the capitulation meeting, explicitly threatened the Dutch delegation with the bombing of Bandung. He subsequently became Chief of the General Affairs Department of the Army Air Force HQ. In 1945, Endo was President of the Aeronautical Ordnance Bureau and President of the Council of Aeronautical Industry. The photo shows Endo after his promotion to lieutenant-general, wearing service dress M1943 (Type 3). (Mainichi Newspapers)

independently and would demonstrate appropriate initiative if necessary. Shoji did indeed do this, but not as anticipated by Imamura. In fact, he acted against explicit orders by attacking the Ciater defensive position on his own, a bold action that was rewarded with success: he breached the heart of the NEI defence in two days and decided the campaign.

Major-General Shoji was sentenced to death in 1949 by the Temporary Courts-Martial at Jakarta for war crimes at Kalidjati, Subang and the Ciater Pass. However, this sentence was converted into a ten-year prison term following an appeal.

**Major-General Saburo Endo (1893–1984)** was the commander of the Imperial Japanese Army Air Service (IJAAS) 3rd Air Division. Endo graduated from the Military Officers School in 1914 and from the Military Staff College in 1922. He became an artillery officer. He gained international experience at the disarmament conference in Geneva in 1927 and the disarmament conference of the League of Nations in 1931. As a staff officer, he was assigned to the North China Area Army in 1937. Endo made the switch to the air force late in his career. He was an aggressive commander. In Java, Endo became annoyed by the slow progress of the 2nd Division and therefore wholeheartedly supported Shoji's decision to attack Bandung. On his own initiative he moved the centre of gravity of the air support given by his 3rd Air Division from the 2nd Division to the Shoji Detachment. He was praised by the Twenty-Fifth Army and the Third Air Force for the conduct of the 3rd Air Division during the Malaya and NEI campaigns.

**Major-General Shizuo Sakaguchi (1887–1947)** became commander of the infantry group of the 56th Division in 1941. For the Southern Offensive, this group was reorganized into the 56th Mixed Infantry Group or Detachment A (Sakaguchi Detachment). Major-General Sakaguchi took part in the entire campaign against the Netherlands East Indies, from Tarakan to Java. In addition to air bases, his unit captured important oil wells and installations. To reach his goal, Sakaguchi was ruthlessly inventive as well: ruthless,

Major-General Shizuo Sakaguchi was the commander of the Infantry Group of 56th Division. He led the Sakaguchi Detachment during the NEI campaign. He was ambitious and inventive, but also ruthless. In 1943, he became a divisional commander in China with promotion to lieutenant-general. He retired from active duty in April 1945. (Public domain)

because he partially executed his threat to kill the RNEI Army garrison and Dutch civilians at Balikpapan when the oil installations were destroyed; and inventive on account of his ability to improvise, as evidenced by the last-minute adjustment of the attack plan at Balikpapan on the basis of new information and the deployment of Indonesian police officers who had defected. For the attack on Bandjermasin, after naval support ceased, he formed a flotilla consisting of small vessels to attack the city from the sea as well. His ambition is evidenced by offering his unit for the invasion of Java, despite it not being part of what was planned.

# ALLIED

**Hein ter Poorten (1887–1968)** was Chief of the General Staff of the RNEI Army from 1939 to 1941. After the fatal plane crash that killed his predecessor, he became commander of the army in the Netherlands East Indies and head of the Department of War (Army Commander) on 23 October 1941. He was promoted to lieutenant-general. Ter Poorten also became ABDA-ARM (i.e. ABDA land forces) commander with the establishment of ABDACOM.

Ter Poorten was born in Buitenzorg (Bogor) in Java in 1887 and was appointed an officer in the artillery of the colonial army in 1908. Ter Poorten was a pioneer in the field of military aviation. He was the first Dutch professional officer to obtain an international flying licence (1911). From 1915 to 1917, he served with the Experimental Flight Unit. Between 1919 and 1922, he attended war studies at the Netherlands Staff College (*Hogere Krijgsschool*). Ter Poorten became inspector of the artillery in 1937. In 1939, the former Army Commander referred to him as 'a particularly gifted officer, a man of original ideas, broad gaze and clear insight ... A powerful chief, smooth and yet deliberate in his decisions'. He was a strong supporter of cooperation with the British in Malaya and Australia, and with the Americans in the Philippines. Ter Poorten wanted to hold onto Singapore and retain Java as the main base for an Allied counter-offensive.

Two months after the outbreak of the war, 54-year-old Ter Poorten was exhausted and had to seek medical attention. As a result, he was not physically and mentally at his best in the period under discussion. Far from being a general optimist, he held no illusions about the chances of victory, and was therefore criticised for being negative. The Army Commander is said not to have shown strong leadership during the fighting. He heavily depended on his chief of staff, Colonel (later Major-General) Rudolph Bakkers.

Relations with the NEI governor general and commander-in-chief Jhr. Tjarda van Starkenborgh Stachouwer, an aristocratic diplomat, were difficult. This was apparent even in the capitulation negotiations with the Japanese in Kalidjati. It was clear to Ter Poorten that Java was lost and that the Japanese expected a general capitulation. The governor general, who was also present

**FAR LEFT**
Lieutenant-General H. ter Poorten had been the chief of staff for two years when he was appointed RNEI Army commander early in October 1941, following the death of his predecessor. He also became ABDA-ARM commander in January 1942. The land areas of operation were spread far apart, so that this command actually embraced little. The burden of the command turned out to be heavy. Ter Poorten looks robust in this photo. However, he became exhausted and was anything but fit when the Japanese Sixteenth Army set foot on Javanese soil. Ter Poorten is dressed in the September 1941 new field dress, but with short sleeves. As an artillery officer, he wears the badge of the artillery on the shoulders of his shirt. (Private collection)

**LEFT**
In this photo, Major-General W. Schilling is still a colonel. His appointment as major-general followed on 30 April 1941. The 52-year-old Schilling was commander of the 1st Division/West Group. He was seen as a competent officer, but he missed several promotions. His name was mentioned as a potential successor to Ter Poorten as chief of the general staff. However, this position passed him by. Schilling declined the offer to lead the counter-attack at Kalidjati-Subang. After the withdrawal from the Priangan Plateau in March 1942, he was the intended commander of the combined West Group and Bandung Group. After his release from captivity in 1945, Schilling was a candidate for army commander, but again was not selected. Instead, he became head of the Netherlands Military Mission in Japan with the rank of lieutenant-general. In 1949, he was given an honourable discharge and returned to the Netherlands. (Museum Bronbeek)

at the initial discussions, wished to negotiate a partial capitulation and reach an agreement on the continuation of civil administration. He reproached Ter Poorten for defeatism.

Ter Poorten went into captivity alongside the governor general. He was liberated on 17 August 1945, in Mukden, China. He felt that he had been made a scapegoat for the defeat of the RNEI Army and the loss of the Netherlands East Indies. Nevertheless, he received an honourable discharge. Ter Poorten died in the Netherlands in 1968.

**Major-General Rudolph Bakkers (1894–1967)**, the son of a European father and an Indonesian mother, became chief of the general staff of the RNEI Army on 27 October 1941. Bakkers became an officer in 1914. Between 1922 and 1925 he attended war studies at the Staff College. He also taught at this institute from 1933 to 1936. As an Indo-European, he forged a brilliant career in a racist colonial society. However, he also experienced discrimination. For example, he was not welcomed into the daily discussions of ABDACOM in lieu of the Army Commander; instead, a chief staff officer was sent.

The 47-year-old Bakkers was described as a 'very high-quality person and tender-hearted'. The latter may have hindered him in taking tough decisions. The death of his wife shortly before the outbreak of war no doubt left its mark on him. It was Bakkers who, in 1941, came up with proposals for a Western organized and armed motorized and mechanized Java army. These plans testify to a sense of vision, but turned out to be too ambitious for the RNEI Army. His advice was always acted on by the Army Commander.

**Major-General Wijbrandus Schilling (1890–1958)** was commander of the 1st Division and 1st Military District from March 1941, and West Group commander from late February 1942. Schilling (aged 52 in January 1942) did not undertake the three-year officer-training course at the Royal Military Academy, but was trained as a non-commissioned officer. Later, he followed a two-year officer's course. Schilling attended the staff college, and from 1929 to 1935 also taught tactics there, along with tactical mapwork. From 1937, Schilling served in staff and operational positions in West Java. As a result, he was highly familiar with his area of operation. The rapid Japanese advance also surprised him. However, he believed that a partial success could be achieved against the Japanese southern axis of advance in West Java.

Schilling was an analytically skilled and knowledgeable officer who combined practical experience in the field with tactical theory. Like his colleagues, however, he lacked combat experience against a modern organized and armed opponent.

**Major-General Jacob Jan Pesman (1888–1950)** was recalled to active duty and given command of the newly formed Bandung Group at the end of February 1942. Pesman graduated from the Royal Military Academy in 1910 as an infantry officer for the colonial army. From 1921 to 1924, he also studied at the Staff College. In 1926 and 1927, Pesman was Regional Military Commander of Riau and Dependencies. In 1939, he became commanding officer of the 1st Division and the 1st Military District. For health reasons, he requested a discharge, granted in April 1941. Bandung Group had to defend the Priangan region in West Java where the RNEI Army's main support services were located. He was also tasked with the counter-attacks on Kalidjati Airfield. After his release from Japanese captivity in 1945, he retired from military service.

Pesman is said to have given 'excellent' leadership to Bandung Group. His relationship with Ter Poorten was apparently difficult. His command was hurriedly formed and lacked cohesion. His HQ was too small and his units were unfamiliar with the terrain. The units were distributed in companies across airfields and positions that blocked access to the Priangan Plateau. The counter-attacks to retake Kalidjati and the defence of the Ciater position lacked coordination and strength. Pesman made hardly any use of the remaining fighter aircraft available to him during daylight hours from the morning of 5 March 1942.

**Major-General Ludolph Hendrik van Oijen (1889–1953)** was commander of the Military Aviation Service. After studying at the Royal Military Academy, he was appointed as an infantry officer in the RNEI Army in 1911. Between 1920 and 1922, he returned to the Royal Military Academy as a teacher. From 1922 to 1925, he took war studies at the Staff College. Back in the Netherlands East Indies, Van Oijen, now a major on the General Staff, took command of the Aviation Service (*Luchtvaartafdeling*) on 29 October 1934. He was not a pilot and had never previously served with this branch. Within the RNEI Army, however, it was customary for an officer of the General Staff to command the Aviation Service. Van Oijen led the

In 1941, Major-General J.J. Pesman retired early, allegedly due to alcohol dependency. Nevertheless, he was tasked with organizing the voluntary territorial Country Guards (*landwachten*). The 54-year-old, corpulent Pesman (right) was restored to active service in February 1942 to command the newly formed Bandung Group. When Major-General Schilling (left) was appointed to command the combined West Group and Bandung Group after the withdrawal on the Priangan Plateau, Pesman resigned. (Netherlands Institute of Military History)

**FAR LEFT**
L.H. van Oijen following his promotion on 15 June 1940 to major-general. Van Oijen was appointed adjutant in ordinary service of Her Majesty the Queen in 1933. The following year he became an adjutant in extraordinary service. From 1934, (although not a pilot) he was commander of the (post-1939 Military) Aviation Service. The 52-year-old Van Oijen witnessed the Japanese air attack on Pearl Harbor on 7 December 1941, while staying there on the return flight from a two-month business trip to the United States and Canada. He did not reach Java until 17 December 1941, after an adventurous journey. In the photo he wears the special uniform of the Aviation Service with, on his right shoulder, the aiguillettes of adjutant of Her Majesty the Queen. (Nationaal Archief, public domain)

**LEFT**
Brigadier A.S. Blackburn was a Victoria Cross holder from World War I. In the interwar years, he was a lawyer and served in the militia. In 1940, he rejoined the army and served as a lieutenant-colonel in the 2/3rd Machine-Gun Battalion, Australian 7th Division in Syria. On 21 February 1942, Blackburn became GOC of all AIF personnel on Java and was promoted to brigadier. He reorganized the various Australian units allotted to ground defence of five airfields around Jakarta into a motorized brigade concentrated at Bogor. He was an aggressive commander and was open to new tactics. He learned from the experience of others in Malaya, and used that knowledge to put up a stubborn defence at Lewiliang. In this photo, Blackburn is a captain. (Australian War Memorial)

transformation of the small Aviation Service into a modernly equipped independent weapon: the Military Aviation Service. He became an inspector of the Military Aviation Service in 1939. Van Oijen witnessed the Japanese air attack on Pearl Harbor on 7 December 1941.

Van Oijen was evacuated to Australia shortly before the RNEI Army in Java surrendered. He became commander of the Netherlands Military Flying School in the United States. In 1943, he was promoted to lieutenant-general and appointed deputy army commander. Van Oijen retired from the military in January 1946.

**Brigadier Arthur Seaforth Blackburn (1892–1960)** was a Victoria Cross holder. He commanded an improvised combat unit on Java known as Blackforce. Blackburn was born in Australia. He fought in World War I as an officer of the Australian Imperial Force (AIF) at Gallipoli and on the Western Front, where he earned his VC. He was discharged in 1917 on medical grounds and returned to civilian life in Australia, but remained on the reserve. In 1940, he rejoined the army as a lieutenant-colonel. Blackburn commanded a machine-gun battalion and saw action in Syria.

His battalion was among the lead elements of the Australian 7th Division to disembark in the Netherlands East Indies. On 21 February 1942, Blackburn was given command of all AIF personnel in Java. He organized his diverse command in a short time into an infantry brigade (reduced). He took the lessons from Malaya to heart when defending Leuwiliang. He deployed his troops in depth and formed a mobile reserve in a counter-encirclement role. Blackburn proved to be an energetic and inventive commander.

# OPPOSING FORCES

## JAPANESE

The Imperial Japanese Army (IJA) and the Imperial Japanese Navy (IJN) worked together in the Imperial General Headquarters (IGHQ). The IGHQ was chaired by the emperor and formed the military and political summit of the army and navy. The IGHQ was not an umbrella headquarters. The armed forces were not subordinated, but had their own parallel organizations. For joint operations, agreement had to be sought between the two armed forces. The resulting compromises were recorded in a written agreement. Consultation between the IGHQ and the government took place in the IGHQ–government liaison conferences. We also find this consultation structure between the IJA and IJN at an operational level. Inter-service competition was particularly strong.

Of its 51 infantry divisions, the IJA made 11 available for the Southern Offensive (Operation *A-Go*), organized into four armies controlled by the new Southern Army (*Nampo Gun*). Three divisions were earmarked for the attack on the Netherlands East Indies. For this purpose, Sixteenth Army was formed under Lieutenant-General Hitoshi Imamura on 6 November 1941. This army consisted of the 2nd Division and the 56th Mixed Infantry Group (Sakaguchi Detachment) of the 56th Division. At a later stage of operations, the 38th Division and 48th Division would be added. With the exception of the 38th, these were Type A1 divisions and handpicked for the task ahead. The 38th Division had experience of swampy terrain in southern China, while the 48th Division was not only motorized but also amphibious-trained. The IJA set up parachute training in December 1940. The airborne 1st Raiding Group witnessed its first combat in the Netherlands East Indies.

Given problems with available shipping, the 11 divisions were significantly reduced in strength before the Southern Offensive from approximately 24,000 to 13,000–14,000 men. Three divisions were motorized. Even with the force reduction, the 2nd Division had to leave the 3rd Battalion, 2nd Field Artillery Regiment in Japan due to a shortage of ships. The assigned divisions were triangular, consisting of the standard infantry group headquarters with three infantry regiments, a field or mountain artillery regiment, a reconnaissance regiment, an engineer regiment, a transport regiment and further support units. The reconnaissance, engineer and transport regiments were actually battalion-size units.

The IJA successfully conducted a daring military offensive. Due to the aggressive and mobile action undertaken, the IJA seized the initiative and kept it for the duration of the entire campaign. Its opponents were not given the opportunity to build an effective defence or to deploy sufficient reinforcements. The Southern Offensive was carried out on an operational level according to the agreed process: acquiring air superiority; conducting an amphibious landing, sometimes in combination with an airborne operation; capturing an airfield; and preparing the airfield, into which army and navy air forces deployed. This process was then repeated. Using this approach, Japan secured its air and naval advantage. The various attack units could support each other if necessary. It kept the Allies off-balance and complicated concentrated counter-action. Amphibious landings occurred shortly after midnight, and were often executed in several places simultaneously. Fortified coastal strips were avoided. After the landing, little time was spent on consolidating the position, with units mostly pushing directly inland. The emphasis was on speed, with advances by road. On Java, the divisions and Sakaguchi Detachment operated along two parallel axes. Tanks led the way, with the infantry behind in trucks. Tactically, the troops were highly disciplined and quick to act. The infantry deployed only after fire contact. In such an event, an attempt was made to immediately eliminate the opponent. If that did not work, an envelopment followed. Threatened with encirclement, the enemy usually broke contact. Cohesion was strictly maintained. Japan's military was well trained. This operational and tactical performance proved to be extremely effective.

The Combined Fleet formed the operational element of the IJN. The fleet was organized into several subfleets. Task forces were formed from the fleets for operational missions. The Southern Task Force was formed for Operation *A-Go* and was the naval equivalent of the Southern Army. During the attack on Malaya and the Philippines – the Phase I operations – it consisted of the Main Unit, Philippines Unit, Malaya Unit, Air Unit and Submarine Unit. During the Phase II operations – the attack on the Netherlands East Indies – most of the Philippines Unit was transferred to the newly formed Netherlands East Indies Unit.

Historically, the IJN focused on fighting a decisive naval battle. In the Southern Offensive, however, the IJN would corner its opponent using advanced air bases. This operational performance was new to the IJN. For the new amphibious and construction tasks, by the end of 1941 the IJN had formed nine battalion-sized Special Landing Forces (SLFs), including two parachute-trained SLFs, and six operational construction units for the expansion of airfields.

The advanced air bases had to be captured from the enemy and made suitable for Japanese operational units. The latter turned out to be more difficult than expected. The airfields usually consisted of grass and were too waterlogged to hold the weight of the aircraft due to the heavy rainfall during the wet season. Also, the runways were often too narrow and too short. For Japanese fighter planes, runways had to be at least 100m wide, 1,000m long and able to support a weight of three tons. For medium-sized, land-based attack aircraft, a length of 1,200m was required. The new construction units comprised ten officers, 20 administrative staff and, depending on the task, up to 3,000 military workers. However, these units lacked modern construction material. The commissioning of captured airfields took longer

This youthful Japanese member of the Special Landing Forces is dressed in the SLF Model 1937 uniform. His weapons comprise the 6.5mm Type 38 (1905) Arisaka repeating rifle with mounted bayonet Model 30 (1897). He carries a set of Model 99 cartridge pouches. Over his shoulders he carries on his right a canteen and on his left a haversack. His helmet has a fabric cover with a camouflage net. The SLF soldiers were not seen by the Japanese as elite troops, but as sailors with a shore posting. (Public domain)

17

IJA and IJN troops committed numerous war crimes during Operation *A-Go*. At Laha Airfield on Ambon, around 340 Australian and Dutch prisoners of war were murdered in four massacres between 1 and 9 February 1942. Their graves were excavated in 1945. The exhumed bodies were wrapped in blankets after identification and reburied with full military honours. (Netherlands Institute of Military History)

than expected. Also, aircraft could not fill up and/or take off when fully armed. This had a negative effect on the deployment of airpower. All this led to the strict timetable running over.

The execution of several naval operations in a short space of time proved to be a great burden for the IJN. It faced a shortage of ships and aircraft to provide all the operations with sufficient escort ships, minesweepers and air support. The IJN was also short on naval landing troops. With some adjustments to the distribution of units, the IJN was largely able to meet these versatile demands.

The IJA and IJN performed ruthlessly during Operation *A-Go*. War crimes occurred regularly. Civilians and prisoners of war, including the wounded, were deliberately murdered in various places.

# RNEI ARMY

The RNEI Army was a colonial force with a twofold task: internal security, and defence against a foreign enemy. This dualism was reflected in its organization, tactics and armament. Small isolated detachments of garrison infantry were stationed in the 'Outer Regions' (*Buitengewesten*) – the islands beyond Java and Madura. These were trained to fight an internal enemy: they served to maintain order and authority. Armament consisted of the 6.5mm M95 repeating carbine and the *klewang* (a sabre). The Java Army (*Javaleger*) was stationed on Java. It mainly fulfilled a defensive role and was therefore intended to fight a possible foreign enemy. Its core comprised four infantry regiments, two artillery regiments and one cavalry regiment.

The RNEI Army was a standing professional army of long-term volunteers. Volunteers from the Netherlands formed the core of the army and counter-balanced the numerical predominance of non-Europeans. The non-Europeans (i.e. Indonesians) were not recruited from all population groups, but from only a few select ethnic groups from the Indonesian archipelago. The proportion of Europeans was increased in wartime by European conscripts. Conscription for Indonesians was only introduced in 1941 under pressure from the external threat. Annual quotas of 3,000 people were expected. In fact, Indonesian conscription was limited to Java, the Minahassa Peninsula (North Sulawesi) and Ambon, and by this point it was a case of too little, too late.

In peace and wartime, the Netherlands East Indies did not have a joint headquarters for land and naval forces. The two lines of command only converged at the governor general as commander-in-chief of the army and fleet. The army and navy had their own chain of command under the Commander of the Army (*Legercommandant*) and the Commander of the Navy (*Commandant Zeemacht*). These commanders headed the Department of War and the Department of Navy respectively. These administrative departments combined the functions of a department of defence, general headquarters, operational command and support organization. During wartime, the operational tasks of the War Department were transferred to the General Headquarters (*Algemeen Hoofdkwartier*) under the Army Commander. The Field Army Headquarters (*Hoofdkwartier Veldleger*) would be formed from the Operations Branch of the General Staff (part of the Department of War) to command the field army.

The chain of command was further complicated by the position of the Royal Netherlands Navy (*Koninklijke Marine*). It was not an NEI institute, but came under the Ministry of Defence in the Netherlands. Although the Commander of the Navy was operationally under the governor general, he was accountable to the Minister of Defence in the Netherlands for his administrative policy. The navy was funded from the Netherlands and NEI budgets. The armed forces also remained physically separate. The General Headquarters was based in Bandung. The HQ of the Royal Netherlands Navy was in Jakarta.

On 5 March 1942, the governor general was released from supreme command by the Netherlands government in London. The governor general would thus be given free reign to continue to administrate the area under the Japanese. This turned out to be wishful thinking.

In the interbellum, the RNEI Army underwent three rounds of austerity cuts: 1922–23, 1927 and 1930–35. From 1936, defence budgets increased again due to the rising international tension in Europe and Asia. The army command formulated the 1936 reinforcement plan. This eight-point programme provided for further reinforcement of the air arm, mechanization of the infantry, increase of firepower for infantry and (coastal) artillery and the filling of gaps in personnel.

The Aviation Service was converted from two reconnaissance squadrons and a fighter squadron with a first-line strength of 18 aircraft in 1936 into the Military Aviation Service, with seven medium bomber squadrons, four fighter squadrons and two reconnaissance squadrons. It had 95 bombers, 99 fighters, 34 reconnaissance aircraft and 155 other aircraft. The mid-level horizontal Glenn Martin B-10/139 WH bomber purchased between 1936 and 1939 was modern at that point, but was considered obsolete by 1941. The WH-3 and WH-3A (61 aircraft) planes still offered decent performance, but their armour and defensive armament was too weak against attacks from Japanese fighters. Instead, 162 North American B-25C-5-NA Mitchell medium bombers were ordered. These aircraft were delivered from February 1942 – too late to join the fight. The RNEI Army's main fighter, the Brewster B-339D (63 aircraft), was in no way inferior to the Nakajima Ki-43-Ia (Oscar), the IJA fighter plane. The Mitsubishi A6M2 (Zeke/Zero), the IJN fighter, was, however, more heavily armed and had tracer ammunition.

In addition to partly obsolete materiel, a lack of trained (technical) personnel was the second weakness of the RNEI Army's air arm. For example, there was no formal combat flight training for fighter pilots. This was due to a shortage of experienced instructors and the lack of effective combat tactics.

The prioritization of the air arm led to a delay in the material modernization of the army. The emphasis was on increasing firepower and mobility. The former was increased with imports of plunging-fire weapons,

At the end of 1941, the RNEI Army's cavalry was reorganized into a mounted squadron and four motorized squadrons. A motorized squadron had a command group, two jeep platoons equipped with Ford GP jeeps and motorcycles, a platoon of armoured cars with four M3A1 (pau W) White Scout Cars and three AC3D (pau S) Alvis-Straussłers and a combat and baggage train. The jeep platoons each included a section of 12.7mm M30 Colt machine guns. The photo probably shows the 2nd Cavalry Squadron at Bandung with the two jeep platoons, the command group in the centre foreground, and to the right the platoon of armoured cars and the radio car of the command group. (Nationaal Archief, Collectie DLC, public domain)

In 1937, the RNEI Army cavalry received 12 Alvis-Straussler AC3D armoured cars. The Alvis-Straussler had a crew of four, and was protected by 5–10mm of armour. Its weaponry consisted of a 12.7mm Colt-Browning machine gun in the turret, a 6.5mm Vickers machine gun for the driver and another 6.5mm Vickers in the vehicle. Four platoons were formed from the 12 armoured cars. In 1941, the platoons were divided among four motorized squadrons. (Beeldbank WW2 – NIOD)

anti-tank and anti-aircraft weapons and machine pistols. Mobility was increased by purchasing jeeps, trucks and armoured cars. Some of the vehicles were civilian vehicles that are requisitioned upon mobilization. Tanks (*vechtwagens*) were also brought into the RNEI Army. In 1939, orders were placed to supply 118 Vickers-Carden-Loyd light tanks and command tanks. When Great Britain blocked the supply of most tanks in 1940, a replacement supplier was found in the Marmon-Herrington Company in the United States. A total of 653 tanks were ordered from there. Only a few tanks were delivered from this order in early 1942. Due to the influx of new weapons and equipment, the RNEI Army was in a permanent state of reorganization between 1936 and 1942.

In terms of personnel strength and armament, a RNEI Army infantry regiment could stand comparison with its Japanese counterpart on most points. However, the RNEI Army was significantly weaker with regard to grenade dischargers and battalion and regimental artillery (see Table 3). The strengths of an RNEI Army and an IJA artillery regiment did not differ much from one another. An NEI regiment of mobile artillery was equipped with 24 7.5cm guns and 12 10.5cm howitzers. A Japanese artillery regiment had 36 7.5cm pieces. With regard to tanks, the Japanese clearly held an advantage. On Java, they deployed 91 medium and light tanks, compared to 40 light tanks for the Allies, comprising seven Marmon-Herrington CTLS-4TA tanks and 17 Vickers-Carden-Loyd M1936 light tanks of the RNEI Army and 16 Vickers-Armstrongs Mk VIB light tanks of the British Army.

In 1927, a minimum strength of two cruisers, eight destroyers and 12 submarines was established for the Royal Netherlands Navy in the

### Table 3: Comparison of weapons

| | Infantry regiment, Japanese standard division[1] | Infantry regiment, RNEI Army |
|---|---|---|
| Strength | 3,843 (2,719) | 3,687 |
| Horses | 710 (203) | 408 |
| Rifles or carbines | 2,131 | 2,879 |
| SMGs | – | 204 |
| LMGs | 112 | 90 |
| Grenade dischargers | 108 | – |
| 81mm mortars | – | 18 |
| MMGs | – | 36 |
| HMGs | 24 | 9 |
| Machine cannons or 20mm anti-tank rifles | – | 12 |
| 37mm or 47mm anti-tank guns | 6 (4) | 6 |
| 70mm battalion guns | 6 | – |
| 75mm regimental guns | 4 | – |

**Note**
1. Numbers given in brackets are figures for the 2nd Division.

Netherlands East Indies. Plans to strengthen the fleet with battleships, battlecruisers or heavy cruisers led to fierce discussion within the navy. There was no unanimity. In 1938, a fleet plan was submitted for the construction of three battlecruisers, among others, but it was not implemented. In 1941, in the Netherlands East Indies the following vessels were present: two light cruisers, a flotilla leader, seven destroyers and 15 submarines. The Naval Aviation Service (*Marine Luchtvaart Dienst*) had 59 flying boats (Dornier Do24K and Consolidated PBY Catalina) and eight tactical reconnaissance planes.

Five heavily armed NEI soldiers in firing positions. In the upper right is an LMG team, comprising gunner and assistant, operating the short-barrelled 6.5mm Madsen M15 'carbine machine gun' (*karabijnmitrailleur*). The two soldiers in the foreground are armed with the 9mm Schmeisser MP 28/II (KNIL M39) sub-machine gun. The soldier at upper right is wearing his gas mask bag in the 'ready' position. (Beeldbank WW2 – NIOD)

The defence of the Netherlands East Indies against a foreign enemy suffered from structural weaknesses. In 1930, an indigenous population of 60 million souls was dominated politically, administratively and economically by 240,000 Europeans. The position of this European top layer was weakened after May 1940 as support from the Netherlands fell away. The Indonesian people concealed nationalistic desires. The US Chief of Naval Operations Harold R. Stark stated in his 12 November 1940 'Memorandum for the Secretary (Plan Dog)': 'This political situation cannot be viewed as in permanent equilibrium. The rulers are unsupported by a home country or by an alliance. Native rebellions have occurred in the past, and may recur in the future.' A retired colonel expressed in a Netherlands East Indies newspaper on 23 July 1940 the idea that 'the vast mass of the population, especially those in Java, may be considered as completely loyal and even attached to the existing authority, as it is now established and organized'. This view turned out to be an *idée fixe*. The Dutch colonial state and thus its army were essentially an occupation force with little support from within Indonesian society.

On a relatively broad scale, in the other regions and in Java, the collapse of colonial rule led to serious looting and arson on occasion, as the Indonesian people seized the opportunity.

## ALLIES

As agreed in the Anglo-Dutch-Australian staff conference in February 1941 and recorded in the Plans for the Employment of Naval and Air Forces (PLENAPS) of 12 November 1941, after the outbreak of hostilities Australia sent air units to the islands of Ambon and Timor in the Netherlands East Indies. No. 13 Squadron RAAF stationed light bomber and coastal reconnaissance aircraft on Ambon and at Namlea on the island of Buru. At Penfoei Airfield on Timor, a flight from No. 2 Squadron RAAF was stationed. For security purposes, three battalion battle groups were formed from the 23rd Infantry Brigade, Australian 8th Division: Lark Force (for Rabaul, New Britain), Gull Force (Ambon) and Sparrow Force (Timor). With these units Australia formed a 'forward observation line'.

These Australian units were part of the all-volunteer Second Australian Imperial Forces (2nd AIF). In their deployment in the Netherlands East Indies, they lacked heavy weapons. Moreover, they were neither trained nor equipped for jungle warfare. The soldiers were dressed in shorts, which were unsuitable for duty in thickly vegetated terrain under tropical conditions. Scratches and cuts on the knees and lower legs led to tropical sores. Malaria prevention was virtually unknown. The result was a high sickness rate and a decline in fighting power. Command relations with the local RNEI Army commanders left much to be desired.

In February 1942, an ad hoc infantry brigade was formed from Australian units and stragglers in Java: Blackforce. Brigadier A.S. Blackburn reorganized three infantry battalions and a supply company (approximately 2,800 men), reinforced with two batteries of the US 2nd Battalion, 131st Field Artillery Regiment and the British B Squadron, 3rd King's Own Hussars with 16 Vickers-Armstrongs Mk VI light tanks. The battalions had only light infantry armament, with three mortars with limited ammunition stocks, and some anti-tank rifles. Blackforce lacked anti-tank guns and anti-tank mines, and a field ambulance was also missing. In contrast, a British signals platoon was added. The core of this unit had gained combat experience in Syria.

Great Britain did not contribute forces until shortly before the fall of Singapore. The British forces in the Netherlands East Indies were mostly not reinforcements but troops withdrawn from Malaya. As a result of the Japanese advance through Malaya and air raids at airfields around Singapore, the RAF and RAAF squadrons were withdrawn to Sumatra and Java from 16 January 1942. British anti-aircraft artillery was deployed for ground-based air defence.

After the loss of South Sumatra, the remaining British forces were reorganized on Java. They consisted of RAF and RAAF squadrons as part of West Group or BRITAIR and Recc Group, the British 16th Anti-Aircraft Brigade and B Squadron, 3rd King's Own Hussars. Four Air Ministry Experimental Station (AMES) units with radar installations were operational at the end of February. In the second half of February, the Royal Navy contributed to the Combined Striking Force.

The United States provided the USAAF's Far East Air Force (FEAF) and the Asiatic Fleet evacuated from the Philippines. The FEAF was first withdrawn to Darwin, northern Australia, but later in December deployed to East Java. The FEAF in Java would eventually consist of 5th Bomber Command and Interceptor Command equipped with modern aircraft. Interceptor Command deployed for the air defence of East Java.

Ships from the Asiatic Fleet participated with success in the maritime defence of the archipelago. On 23 and 24 December 1941, Patrol Wing 10 was withdrawn from the Philippines with eight Catalina US Navy flying boats relocated to Halong, Ambon.

On 11 January 1942, the HQ 26th Field Artillery Brigade and 2nd Battalion, 131st Field Artillery Regiment arrived in Surabaya from the USA (part of the Pensacola Convoy). The latter was a field artillery battalion of the Texas National Guard and mobilized in late 1940. It arrived in Java at full strength, but with half the motor transport and none of the 14 organic .50-cal. heavy machine guns. The unit was also equipped with 12 M2A2 75mm truck-drawn guns shortly before departure from the United States. No shooting practice had yet been held with the new artillery. Of the eight American SCR-268 radar sets sent, two were operational at the end of January 1942.

# ORDERS OF BATTLE

## JAPANESE

### SOUTHERN ARMY (GENERAL HISAICHI TERAUCHI)[1]

**Sixteenth Army (Lieutenant-General Hitoshi Imamura)**
2nd Division (Lieutenant-General Masao Maruyama)
    4th Infantry Regiment
    16th Infantry Regiment
    29th Infantry Regiment
    2nd Reconnaissance Regiment
    2nd Field Artillery Regiment
    2nd Engineer Regiment
    2nd Transport Regiment
    Signal, ordnance and medical units
    Total: 13,755 men, 1,335 horses and 586 motor vehicles
38th Division (Lieutenant-General Tadayoshi Sano)[2]
    239th Infantry Regiment
    38th Mountain Artillery Regiment
    38th Engineer Regiment
    38th Transport Regiment
    Signal, ordnance and medical units
    Total: 12,360 men, 1,910 horses
    Eastern Detachment (Major-General Takeo Ito)[3]
        228th Infantry Regiment
        Light Armoured Car Unit
        2nd Battalion, 38th Mountain Artillery Regiment
        Signal, ordnance and medical units
        Total: 5,300 men, 400 horses and 110 motor vehicles
    Shoji Detachment (Colonel Toshishige Shoji)[4]
        230th Infantry Regiment (reduced)
        1st Company, 4th Tank Regiment
        3rd Battalion, 38th Mountain Artillery Regiment
        Signal, ordnance and medical units
        Airfield Unit (core 24th Airfield Battalion)
        Total: c. 3,000 men
48th Division (Lieutenant-General Yuitsu Tsuchihashi)
    1st Formosan Infantry Regiment[5]
    2nd Formosan Infantry Regiment
    47th Infantry Regiment
    48th Reconnaissance Regiment
    48th Mountain Artillery Regiment
    48th Engineer Regiment
    48th Transport Regiment
    Signal, ordnance and medical units
    Total: 12,893 men, 975 horses and 784 motor vehicles
Detachment A, 56th Mixed Infantry Group (Major-General Shizuo Sakaguchi)
    146th Infantry Regiment
    56th Infantry Group Armoured Car Unit
    1st Battalion, 56th Field Artillery Regiment
    Total: 5,200 men, 1,200 horses and 100 motor vehicles

**Sixteenth Army troops**
8th Tank Regiment
2nd Tank Regiment (reduced)
17th Field Heavy Artillery Regiment
16th Anti-Aircraft Artillery Regiment
23rd Anti-Aircraft Artillery Regiment (reduced)
1st Independent Engineer Regiment
3rd Independent Engineer Regiment
15th Telegraph Regiment
28th Motor Transport Regiment
Field Military Police, Field Gas, Railway, Radio, Telegraphy, Bridge-Building, Water Supply and Purification units

**Table 4: Detachments**

| Detachment | Alternative name | Parent unit | Campaign | Objective |
|---|---|---|---|---|
| Detachment A | Sakaguchi Detachment | 56th Division | NEI | Borneo and Celebes |
| Detachment B | Eastern Detachment or Ito Detachment | 38th Division | NEI | Ambon and Timor |
| Detachment C | Tanaka, Kanno | 48th Division | Philippines | Aparri, Vigan and Laoag |
| Detachment D | Miura Detachment | 16th Division | Philippines | Davao |
| Detachment E | Kimura Detachment | 16th Division | Philippines | Legaspi |
| Detachment F | Kawaguchi Detachment | 18th Division | British Borneo | Miri and Kuching |
| Detachment G | | 18th Division | Malaya | Siam |
| Detachment H | | 55th Division | Malaya | Siam |
| Detachment I | South Seas Detachment or Horii Detachment | 55th Division | Pacific | Guam |

### THIRD AIR FORCE (LIEUTENANT-GENERAL MICHIO SUGAWARA)

81st Air Group (18 Army Type 97 and Type 100 command reconnaissance aircraft)
98th Air Group (seven Army Type 97 heavy bombers)
1st Raiding Group (Colonel Seiichi Kume)[6]
    1st Raiding Regiment
    2nd Raiding Regiment
    Raiding Air Group (36 transport aircraft)[7]
3rd Air Division (Major-General Saburo Endo)
    27th Air Group (36 Army Type 99 assault aircraft)
    75th Air Group (27 Army Type 99 twin-engined light bombers)
    90th Air Group (27 Army Type 99 twin-engined light bombers)
    59th Air Group (24 Army Type 1 fighters)
    50th Independent Squadron (Army Type 97 and Type 100 command reconnaissance aircraft)
7th Air Division (Major-General Kenji Yamamoto)
    64th Air Group (36 Army Type 1 fighters)
    12th Air Group (27 heavy bombers)
    60th Air Group (27 heavy bombers)
    51st Independent Squadron (command reconnaissance aircraft)
12th Air Division
    1st Air Group (36 Army Type 97 fighters)
    11th Air Group (36 Army Type 97 fighters)
    47th Independent Squadron (command reconnaissance aircraft)

---

1 Southern Army was comparable in size to an army group.
2 The 38th Division was deployed in three separate regimental battle groups in the NEI campaign.
3 This unit was part of 38th Division.
4 Also part of 38th Division.
5 Sometimes referred to as the Taiwan Infantry Regiment.
6 Airborne unit.
7 During raiding operations, it was reinforced with the 12th Transport Squadron.

## IMPERIAL JAPANESE NAVY

(Phase II operations, from 26 December 1941)
**Southern Task Force (Vice Admiral Nobutake Kondo) (C-in-C Second Fleet)**
**Netherlands East Indies Unit (Vice Admiral Ibo Takahashi) (C-in-C Third Fleet)**
Main Unit
    16th Cruiser Division (minus 2nd Section)
Western Attack Unit
    1st Escort Unit (4th Destroyer Squadron (reduced), part of 2nd Base Force, 2nd Kure SLF (reduced))
    2nd Base Unit (2nd Base Force (reduced))
    1st Air Unit (12th Seaplane Tender Division (*Sanyo Maru*, *Sanuki Maru*)
    3rd Escort Unit (5th Destroyer Squadron)
Eastern Attack Unit
    Support Unit (5th Cruiser Division, 2nd Section of 6th Destroyer Division)
    2nd Escort Unit (2nd Destroyer Squadron (reduced), 1st Kure SLF (reduced), Sasebo Combined SLF (reduced))
    1st Base Unit (1st Base Force (reduced))
    2nd Air Unit (11th Seaplane Tender Division (*Chitose*, *Mizuho*)
Attached Units (1st, 2nd, 3rd, 5th and 6th Construction units)
Air Unit (Vice Admiral Nishizo Tsukahara) (C-in-C 11th Air Fleet)
    1st Air Raid Unit (21st Air Flotilla) (Rear Admiral Takeo Tada)
        Kanoya Air Group (detachment) (25 Navy Type 1 land-based attack aircraft)
        Toko Air Group (18 Navy Type 97 flying boats)
        1st Air Group (39 Navy Type 96 land-based attack aircraft)
        1001 Unit (28 Navy Type 96 transport aircraft)
        1st Yokosuka Special Landing Force
        3rd Yokosuka Special Landing Force
    2nd Air Raid Unit (23rd Air Flotilla) (Rear Admiral Ryozo Takenaka)
        Takao Air Group (61 Navy Type 1 land-based attack aircraft)
        Tainan Air Group (c. 12 Navy Type 0 fighter aircraft)
        3rd Air Group (c. 20 Navy Type 0 fighter aircraft)
    Carrier-based Air Unit (2nd Carrier Division)
Submarine Unit A
    6th Submarine Squadron
Submarine Unit B
    5th Submarine Squadron (from Malaya Unit)

The 11th Air Fleet was made up of the 21st, 22nd and 23rd Air flotillas. The 22nd Air Flotilla was assigned to the Malaya Unit. Its commander was Rear Admiral Sadaichi Matsunaga. It consisted of the following units:
    Genzan Air Group (36 land-based attack aircraft)
    Mihoro Air Group (36 land-based attack aircraft)
    Yamada Unit (30 Navy Type 0 fighter aircraft, six Navy Type 98 reconnaissance aircraft)

British Borneo was assigned to Detachment F (Kawaguchi Detachment). This detachment also operated in north-west Borneo, under the codename Operation B. This unit was part of the 18th Division in French Indochina. The division was under the direct control of the Southern Army.
Detachment F (Kawaguchi Detachment) (Major-General Kiyotake Kawaguchi)
    124th Infantry Regiment
    Signal, ordnance and medical units
    2nd Yokosuka Special Landing Force

**Table 5: Japanese aircraft names**

| Type designation | Service branch | Aircraft | Allied codename |
|---|---|---|---|
| Navy Type 1 land-based attack aircraft | Navy | Mitsubishi G4M | Betty |
| Navy Type 96 land-based attack aircraft | Navy | Mitsubishi G3M | Nell |
| Navy Type 96 transport aircraft | Navy | Yokosuka L3Y | Tina |
| Navy Type 0 fighter aircraft | Navy | Mitsubishi A6M | Zeke |
| Navy Type 98 reconnaissance aircraft | Navy | Mitsubishi C5M | Norma |
| Navy Type 97 large flying boat | Navy | Kawanishi H6K | Mavis |
| Army Type 99 assault aircraft | Army | Mitsubishi Ki-51 | Sonia |
| Army Type 97 fighter | Army | Nakajima Ki-27 | Nate |
| Army Type 1 fighter | Army | Nakajima Ki-43 Hayabusa | Oscar |
| Army Type 99 twin-engined light bomber | Army | Kawasaki Ki-48 | Lilly |
| Army Type 97 heavy bomber | Army | Mitsubishi Ki-21 | Sally |
| Army Type 97 command reconnaissance aircraft | Army | Mitsubishi Ki-15 | Norma |
| Army Type 100 command reconnaissance aircraft | Army | Mitsubishi Ki-46 | Dinah |

# NETHERLANDS EAST INDIES

## RNEI ARMY

(organization post-mobilization in December 1941)
**General Headquarters**
**Java Army**
1st Division, 2nd Division, 3rd Division, 1st Recon Squadron and 2nd Recon Squadron (Military Aviation Service, RNEI Army)
**Military Aviation Service**
Military Aviation Command (airfields, radio stations, 1st through to 5th Aircraft groups, 4th Recon Squadron, Commander Air Forces Ambon II, Commander Air Forces Samarinda II, Commander Air Forces Singkawang II and Military Aviation Inspectorate
**Territorial commands**
Aceh and Eastern Sumatra, West Sumatra, Riau and Dependencies, Palembang and Djambi, West Borneo, South and East Borneo, Celebes and Menado, Timor, Moluccas
**Troop commands**
Tarakan, Balikpapan, Samarinda
RNEI Army strength

| | |
|---|---:|
| **Java Army** | **93,947** |
|     1st Division | 16,782 |
|     2nd Division | 11,924 |
|     3rd Division | 15,361 |
|     Coastal detachments | 1,330 |
|     Other territorial troops | 11,300 |
|     Support troops | 28,000 |
|     Aviation, medical | 3,250 |
|     Indonesian militia | 6,000 |
| **Outer Regions** | **19,250** |
|     Sumatra | 9,920 |
|     Riau and Banka | 690 |
|     Borneo | 3,400 |
|     Sulawesi | 3,050 |
|     Ambon | 1,640 |
|     Timor | 550 |
| **Total** | **113,197** |

**Java Army (as at 22 February 1942)**
**General Headquarters (Lieutenant-General H. ter Poorten)**
**Strategic Reserve**
2nd Infantry Regiment (9th Infantry Battalion; 14th Infantry Battalion; 15th Infantry Battalion; 10th Company, 2nd Infantry Regiment; 2nd Anti-Tank and Anti-Aircraft Company)
1st Mountain Artillery Battalion, Mobile Unit[8]
1st Recon Squadron (MAS) and 2nd Recon Squadron (Military Aviation Service, RNEI Army)
**West Group (Major-General W. Schilling)**
1st Infantry Regiment (10th Infantry Battalion; 11th Infantry Battalion; 12th Infantry Battalion; 10th Company, 1st Infantry Regiment; 1st Anti-Tank and Anti-Aircraft Company)
Blackforce (1st Infantry Battalion; 2nd Infantry Battalion; 3rd Infantry Battalion (reduced); US 2nd Battalion, 131st Field Artillery Regiment (reduced); British B Squadron, 3rd King's Own Hussars)
1st Cavalry Squadron, 5th Cavalry Squadron, 1st Howitzer Battalion, 1st Engineer Battalion
Jakarta-Tanjung Priok Coastal Front
**Bandung Group (Major-General J.J. Pesman)**
4th Infantry Regiment (1st Infantry Battalion; 2nd Infantry Battalion; 5th Infantry Battalion; 4th Infantry Battalion (added); 10th Company, 4th Infantry Regiment; 4th Anti-Tank and Anti-Aircraft Company)
2nd Cavalry Squadron, 2nd Mountain Artillery Battalion, 2nd Field Artillery Battalion, 7th Mountain Battery, 3rd Engineer Battalion
**2nd Division (Major-General P.A. Cox)**
South Group (Left-Half 21st Infantry Battalion, Right-Half 21st Infantry Battalion, Mangku Negoro Battalion)
4th Cavalry Squadron, Life Guards Cavalry Squadron, 4th Engineer Battalion (reduced)
Cilacap Detachment (two infantry companies, one MMG and mortar unit, three coastal artillery batteries, one field artillery battery, two AA MG platoons)
Territorial troops
**3rd Division (Major-General G.A. Ilgen)**
6th Infantry Regiment (3rd Infantry Battalion; 8th Infantry Battalion; 13th Infantry Battalion; 10th Company, 6th Infantry Regiment; 6th Anti-Tank and Anti-Aircraft Company)
3rd Cavalry Squadron, 6th Cavalry Squadron, 1st Field Artillery Battalion, 6th Field Artillery Battalion; US Battery E, 2nd Battalion, 131st Field Artillery Regiment; 2nd Engineer Battalion, Naval Battalion
Surabaya Security Force (Coastal Artillery Battalion, 2nd Landstorm; 1st, 2nd, 3rd and 4th Barisan (Madurese auxiliary troops))
Territorial troops

## JAVA AIR COMMAND (MAJOR-GENERAL L.H. VAN OIJEN)[9]

**West Group or BRITAIR**
No. 242 (Fighter) Squadron RAF (15 Hurricanes)
No. 605 (Fighter) Squadron RAF (six Hurricanes)
No. 1 (General Reconnaissance) Squadron RAAF (20 Hudson IIs and Hudson IIIs of which five serviceable)
No. 84 (Bomber) Squadron RAF and No. 211 (Bomber) Squadron RAF (26 Blenheims, five serviceable)
**Military Aviation Service Command**
1st Aircraft Group and 2nd Aircraft Group (six Glenn Martins)
3rd Aircraft Group (13 Glenn Martins)
4th Aircraft Group (four Curtiss Interceptor fighter aircraft and 11 Hurricanes)
5th Aircraft Group (12 Brewsters and two Curtiss Hawk fighter aircraft)
**East Group**
17th Pursuit Squadron (eight Curtiss P-40s)
7th Bombardment Group and 19th Bombardment Group (six B-17 and one LB-30 heavy bombers)
27th Bombardment Group (four Douglas A-24 dive-bombers)

**Reconnaissance Group**
2nd Aircraft Squadron, 5th Aircraft Squadron, 6th Aircraft Squadron, 7th Aircraft Squadron, 8th Aircraft Squadron, 16th Aircraft Squadron, 17th Aircraft Squadron, 18th Aircraft Squadron, No. 205 (Flying Boat) Squadron, Patrol Wing 10
**Air Defence Jakarta Control Sector**
1st Anti-Aircraft Battalion; 242nd Battery, 48th Light Anti-Aircraft Regiment (RA); 239th Battery, 77th Heavy Anti-Aircraft Regiment (RA)
**Bandung Air Defence Command**
3rd Anti-Aircraft Battalion; 69th Battery, 21st Light Anti-Aircraft Regiment (RA); 49th and 95th batteries, 48th Light Anti-Aircraft Regiment (RA)
**Surabaya Air Defence Command**
2nd Anti-Aircraft Battalion, 48th Battery, 21st Light Anti-Aircraft Regiment (RA); 240th and 241st batteries, 77th Heavy Anti-Aircraft Regiment (RA)
**Combined Operations and Intelligence Centre (COIC)**

## ROYAL NETHERLANDS NAVY

**Navy Command (Vice Admiral C.E.L. Helfrich)**
**Squadron (Rear Admiral K.W.F.M. Doorman)**
HNLMS *Java*, HNLMS *De Ruyter* (light cruisers), HNLMS *Tromp* (flotilla leader)
1st Destroyer Division
    1st Group: HNLMS *Van Ghent*, HNLMS *Witte de With*, HNLMS *Kortenaer*
    2nd Group: HNLMS *Piet Hein*, HNLMS *Banckert*
    3rd Group: HNLMS *Evertsen*, HNLMS *Van Nes*
Submarine Flotilla
    1st Submarine Division: HNLMS *O 16*, HNLMS *K XVII*, HNLMS *K XVIII*
    2nd Submarine Division: HNLMS *K IX*, HNLMS *K XI*, HNLMS *K XII*, HNLMS *K XIII*
    3rd Submarine Division: HNLMS *K XIV*, HNLMS *K XV*, HNLMS *K XVI*
    4th Submarine Division: HNLMS *O 19*, HNLMS *O 20*, HNLMS *K X*
**Navy Command at Surabaya (Captain P. Koenraad)**
**Naval Aviation Service (Captain G.G. Bozuwa)**
1st through to 18th Aircraft squadrons

| Table 6: Royal Netherlands Navy personnel in the NEI, 1940 | |
|---|---|
| Category | Quantity |
| Officers | 403 |
| Petty officers and men | 3,091[1] |
| Reserve officers | 14 |
| Militia NCOs and enlisted men | 449 |
| Corps of Indonesian Sailors (*Korps Inlandse Schepelingen*) | 1,862 |
| **Total** | **5,819** |

Note:
[1] Including 351 marines.

---

8 According to some sources, part of Bandung Group.
9 FEAF aircraft numbers given are for 26 February 1942.

# Southern Army operational plan and the Iwakuni Agreement

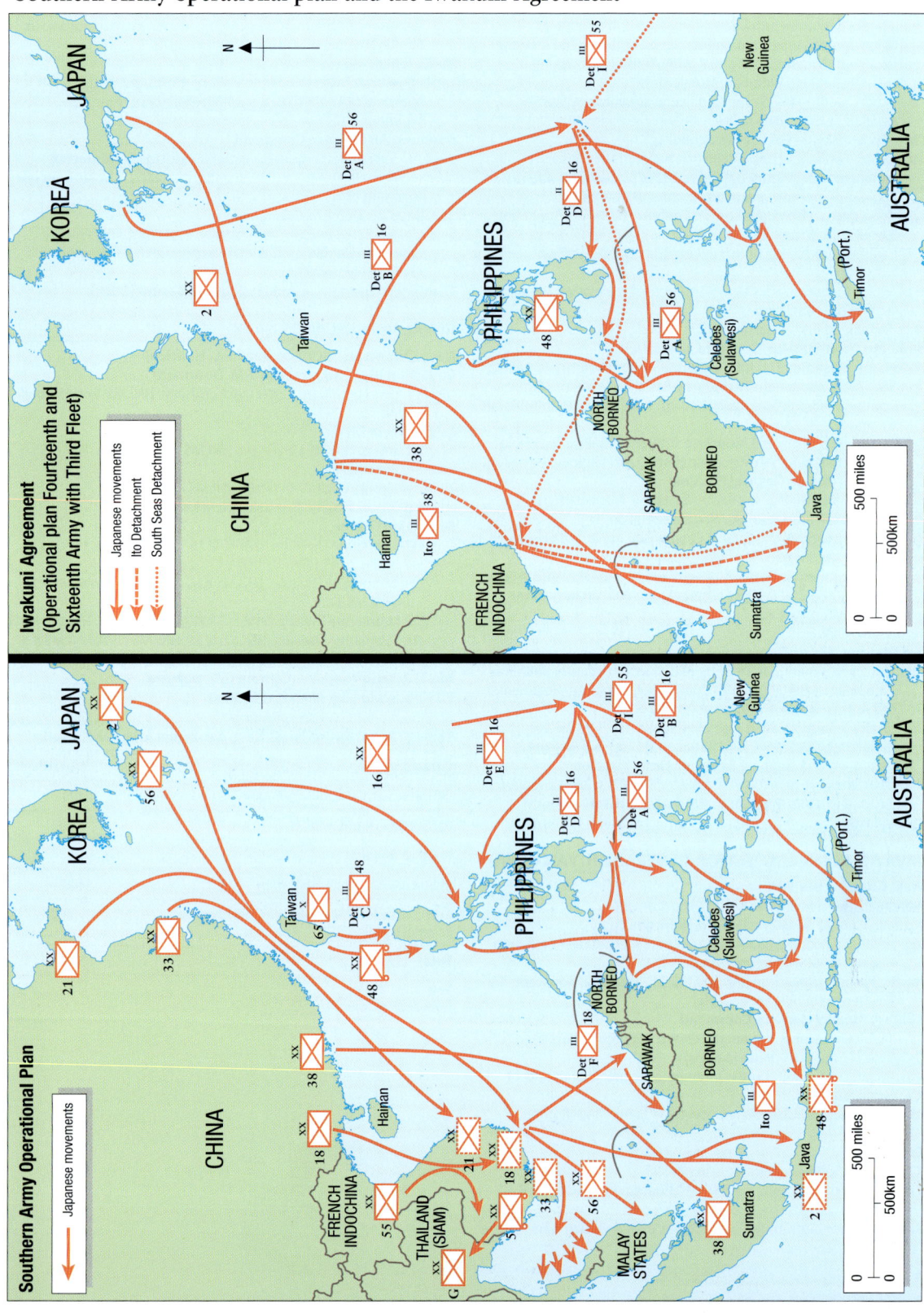

# OPPOSING PLANS

## JAPANESE

The Netherlands East Indies did not attract the interest of Japan's armed forces until the second half of the 1930s. After the occupation of the Netherlands by Germany in May 1940, the IJA and IJN began a joint study into simultaneous operations against four enemies: the United States, Great Britain, the Netherlands and China. After a slow start, this accelerated from April 1941. It was now clear that a peaceful submission of the Netherlands East Indies was not possible. In mid-1941, concrete plans had already been formed.

The IJN planned a 'clockwise advance'. This plan envisioned the conquest of the Philippines from the north by two divisions in two months. Java would then also be taken with two divisions. Next, Singapore would be captured in an envelopment from Sumatra to the south, and from Malaya to the north. The IJA, on the other hand, favoured a 'counter-clockwise advance'. It wished to capture Singapore with a rapid advance. It would block British reinforcements and significantly shorten the turnaround time of the entire operation. This attack would take place simultaneously with the offensive against the Philippines. This meant an attack on both flanks, Malaya and the Philippines, which would then meet on Java.

In the Tokyo Agreement of 10 November 1941, the Southern Army on the one hand, and the Combined Fleet and Southern Task Force on the other, laid down their plans on paper. In the Iwakuni Agreement, both armed forces reached agreement about the Philippines and the Netherlands East Indies.

**Table 7: The schedule for Operation *H*: the Tokyo Agreement**

| Day of start of landing (X day = start of the war) | Key area to capture | Assembly point |
|---|---|---|
| X + 23 | Menado | Palau |
| X + 25 | Tarakan | Palau |
| X + 35 | Kendari | Menado |
| X + 35 | Balikpapan | Tarakan |
| X + 45 | Makassar | Kendari |
| X + 50 | Bandjermasin | Balikpapan |
| X + 60 | Ambon and Kupang | Palau |
| X + 80 | Java, Sumatra | Hong Kong for the capture of Sumatra, Manila for eastern Java, Taiwan and Hong Kong for western Java |

The IJN was allocated the clockwise advance, and the IJA the counter-clockwise one.

Previously, on 10 October 1941, the IJA informed Emperor Hirohito that the capture of most of the key areas in the south was possible in about five months (150 days). This date was then finalized. The IJA and IJN agreed the timeframe given in Table 7 for the attack on the Netherlands East Indies: codename Operation *H*.

The main objective and capstone of the Southern Offensive, Operation *A-Go*, was the conquest of oil wells and the oil refineries in the Netherlands East Indies. The NEI campaign depended heavily on the success of Japanese operations elsewhere in South-East Asia. This was primarily based on the results of the surprise attack on the US fleet in Hawaii. The relocation of the US Battle Force (reorganized into the US Atlantic Fleet and US Pacific Fleet on 1 February 1941) to Hawaii was considered a significant deterrent by the Americans, but had also brought this fleet within reach of the Japanese fleet. The attack was supposed to disable the Pacific Fleet for at least six months. The Pacific Fleet would no longer be able to thwart the conquest of South-East Asia. The operational plan subsequently provided for the conquest and use of Malaya, British Borneo and the Philippines as a springboard for the attack on the Netherlands East Indies. The success of the Japanese attack on these areas was therefore a precondition for the conquest of the NEI. These operations affected the Netherlands East Indies campaign in a further way. A large part of the IJN and IJA units destined for the Netherlands East Indies were deployed in previous operations in China and the Philippines. These only became available after Hong Kong and Manila were conquered. The entire outcome of the Southern Offensive would depend on widespread coordination between land, sea and air units.

There was no question of the element of surprise in the operations against the Netherlands East Indies. After all, this had evaporated with the operations against Malaya, British Borneo and the Philippines. In addition, Java might have in the meantime received American and British reinforcements. The enormous distances were a further complicating factor. The many dependencies made the Southern Offensive an extremely risky operation. A further risk was the often faulty intelligence on which the Japanese were forced to base their operational plans.

The Japanese did not think highly of the combat power of the RNEI Army. The indigenous troops in particular were considered to lack fighting spirit. They expected to conquer Java in about a week.

**Table 8: Japanese operational codenames**

| | |
|---|---|
| Operation *A-Go* | Southern Offensive |
| Operation *B* | British Borneo |
| Operation *E* | Malaya |
| Operation *H* | Java |
| Operation *L* | Bangka and Palembang |
| Operation *M* | Philippines |
| Operation *Q* | landing at Kuantan, cancelled |
| Operation *S* | landing at Endau, cancelled |
| Operation *T* | northern Sumatra invasion |
| Operation *Z* | air campaign against Java |

# NETHERLANDS EAST INDIES

From 1913 onwards, the Netherlands considered Japan as a potential enemy. Japan pursued political and economic expansion, and it had the means – a powerful fleet and army – to do so. The Netherlands expected that Japan's striving for an extension of its authority could not be achieved on the Asian mainland. It therefore had already taken into account that 'Japan will turn to the South'.

The Netherlands East Indies consisted of a long chain of many islands. For the defence of this archipelago, the preservation of air superiority and control of the sealanes was essential. A significant air force and fleet could prevent an enemy from acquiring the air and naval bases. The great distances and fragmented shape of the archipelago prevented coordinated land defence. It gave an attacker with air and naval superiority the opportunity to neutralize a strongly defended island by capturing a supporting location on another island. Java was the main island and the NEI administrative centre, and had by far the most inhabitants. Its island form was narrow and elongated. Its strategic locations were also spread throughout the island. The administrative centre was in West Java, and the naval base in East Java. This called for a robust defence, but at the same time made a concentrated defence of the main island extremely difficult.

Until around 1900, the defence of the NEI was based on the defence of Java. New Principles of Defence (*Defensiegrondslagen*) were established in 1927. This new defensive doctrine broke with the previous one in two key areas. Protecting the Netherlands East Indies no longer focused on defence, but instead on maintaining neutrality. The Netherlands East Indies was no longer to fear an attack aimed at conquest; rather, it was to guard against a *coup de main*. The defensive plan was therefore primarily aimed at maintaining Dutch authority in the NEI colony. The second point of divergence from the former plan was that the defence was no longer limited to Java. The Outer Regions were included in the doctrine. Tarakan and Balikpapan were identified as particularly vulnerable points due to the extraction and refining of petroleum there. The RNEI Army was responsible for maintaining neutrality in Java with the support of the Royal Netherlands Navy. In the Outer Regions, this task was assigned to the navy, with support in some locations from the army. If the NEI unexpectedly became involved in an armed conflict between the major powers, resistance was to be offered until help from a foreign ally or allies was forthcoming. In fact, with the Principles of Defence 1927, the Netherlands acknowledged that it did not have the means to successfully defend the Netherlands East Indies independently against Japanese aggression.

The 1927 Principles of Defence were particularly flawed regarding the threat assessment and the eventual dependence on foreign (viz. British and American) support. The support from a supposed alliance lay beyond the Netherlands' control. The Washington Conference of 1921–22 was said to have relaxed tensions in the Pacific. According to the RNEI Army, nothing could be further from the truth. The agreed partial ban on the construction of maritime bases and the development of the naval base in Singapore had only increased the strategic importance of the Netherlands East Indies. However, preservation of the NEI was a priority for neither Great Britain nor the United States. Firstly, Britain's priorities lay in the Far East with India and Singapore. Secondly, Britain lacked the required resources. Due to the war in Europe, it was unable to send a significant naval force to Singapore.

# RNEI Army locations

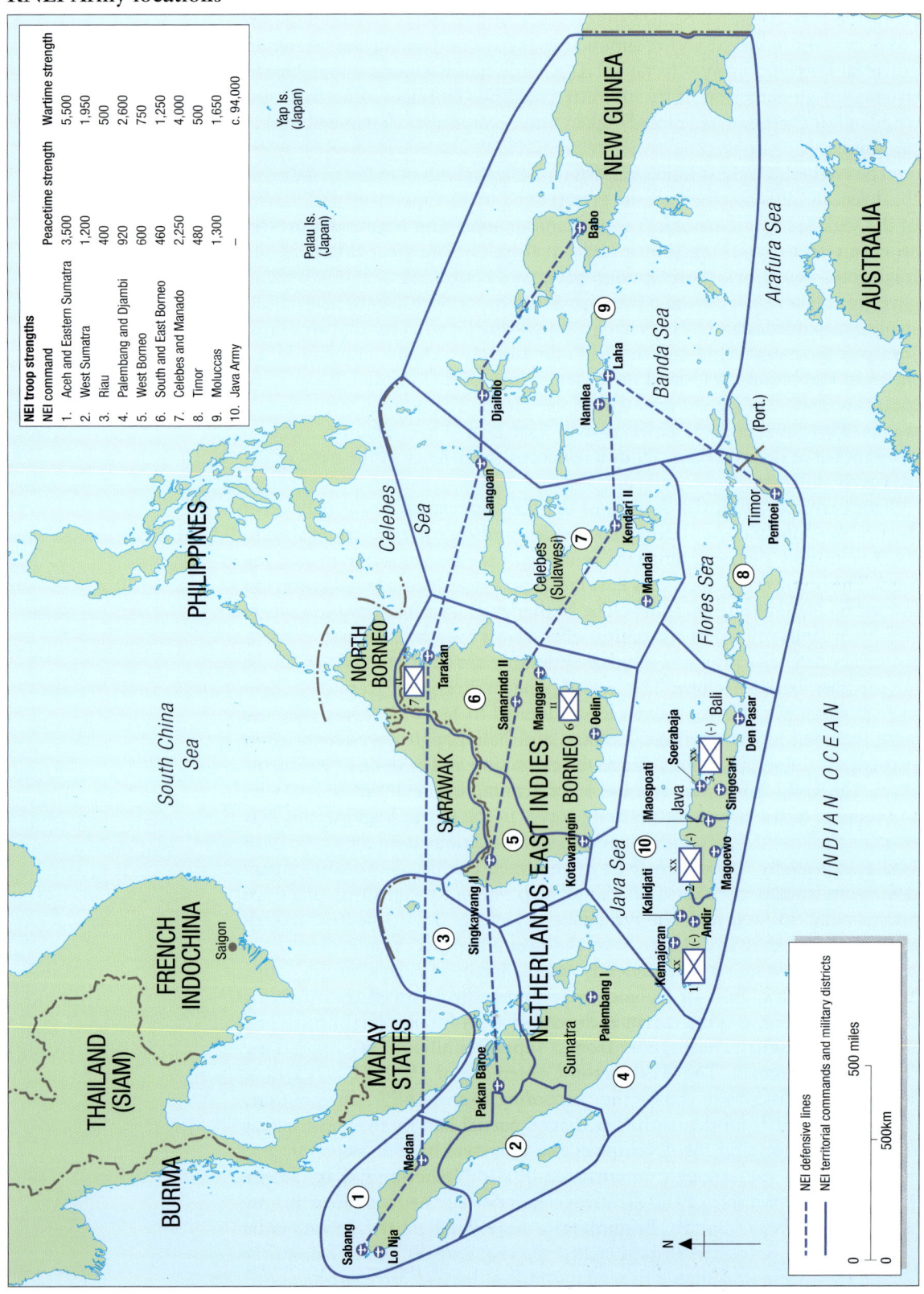

With that, the cornerstone of British defence in the Far East was removed. Britain's position was so weak that, according to the historian H.P. Willmott, 'the British regarded the Dutch not so much as a weak ally facing a common threat, an ally that should be helped, but as a force of support that could be tapped in an effort to buttress Britain's own position' (1982, p. 121). On the list of priorities of the United States were Pearl Harbor, Australia, the Philippines and keeping nationalist China at war. For both these allies, Australia was essential for the reconquest of South-East Asia. Ultimately, the Netherlands East Indies was left to fend for itself.

The RNEI Army leadership disagreed with the underlying assumption of the 1927 Principles of Defence. In the event of a war in the Pacific, the RNEI Army expected to face a targeted attack of conquest against Java, on account of its naval base and oil sites. Given the size of the archipelago and the available resources, the RNEI Army leadership opted for the territorial defence of:

1. Java with the seat of government, naval base and key army and navy institutions;
2. Naval and aircraft support centres in the Outer Regions;
3. The major areas involved in the extraction of strategic raw materials.

The RNEI Army developed an operational doctrine of indirect coastal defence in breadth and depth using horizontal bombers. The air arm was the first line of defence, seeking to prevent an enemy transport fleet from reaching Java. The navy formed the second line of defence, and the army the third. The bombers were intended to attack transport ships ferrying landing troops, not Japanese warships. 'Only landing troops can occupy a support point in our Archipelago. Warships never! ... A warship is fought with a warship, not an airplane.'[10] This demonstrates that the full potential of the air arm had yet to be realized.

The required airfields were constructed in the Outer Regions. These airfields formed three lines of resistance. The outer one ran from Sabang and Medan in Sumatra over Tarakan in Borneo and Langoan (Menado) in Sulawesi to Babo in Western New Guinea. The second line was formed by the airfields Pakan Baroe on Sumatra, Singkawang II and Samarinda II on Borneo, Kendari II on Sulawesi, Ambon II and ending at Kupang on Timor. Palembang I Airfield in Sumatra, the airfields in Java and Den Pasar in Bali formed a final resistance line. In peacetime, the aircraft groups were stationed in Java. Allocation of aircraft to the Outer Regions was temporary and on a secondment basis.

The Royal Netherlands Navy considered the new role of the Military Aviation Service to be in contradiction with the 1927 principles. It pointed to the risk that the airfields could be captured by the enemy and used for an attack on Java. The RNEI Army planned to reduce this risk by constructing the airfields inland and not on the coast, and by preparing for their destruction if need be. Some of the airfields were constructed in secret. For a long time, the Japanese were unaware of the existence of Singkawang II, Samarinda II and Palembang II airfields. However, the navy would be proved correct.

After 1940, the primary task of a number of detachments in the Outer Regions became the defence of the airfields and/or oil ports and oil installations. Maintaining order and peace became a secondary priority. Numerous

---

10 Comment in the margin by NL-HaNA, Koloniën/Geheim archief, 2.10.36.51, inv.nr. 493, V. 11 juni 1937, Lr. L14, Letter CZM to GG, Batavia, 14 December 1936.

The RNEI Army Chief of the General Staff, Colonel R. Bakkers, seated at his desk in the War Department in December 1941, with from left to right Lieutenant-Colonel W.P. van Veen, Deputy, and Lieutenant-Colonel P.G. Mantel, Head of Section III (Defence). Colonel Bakkers was promoted to major-general on 19 February 1942. For office work, following the mobilization, the white undress uniform was replaced with the grey-green field uniform. (Museum Bronbeek)

detachments were disbanded or downsized. The direct defence of airfields was organized in a uniform manner following the 1941 mobilization. This comprised two to three pillboxes with machine guns for covering the airfield and light machine guns to counter air targets; three armoured personel carriers (*overvalwagen*) with light machine guns; and three to four infantry brigades (each comprising a section of 15 men). The airfields were to serve as final redoubts. In 1935, field battalions, albeit with modified organizations and armaments, were transferred from Java to the oil island of Tarakan (7th Infantry Battalion) and the oil port of Balikpapan (6th Infantry Battalion). If called for, these key sites were to be destroyed to prevent them falling into an attacker's hands. Following that, the infantry were to engage in guerrilla warfare. The numerous small, scattered and isolated garrisons had no chance of outside help. They would be bypassed or overwhelmed by superior Japanese forces.

In accordance with the 1927 Principles of Defence, in 1935 the RNEI Army planned to concentrate most of the field army on Java following the outbreak of war, in order to defend Surabaya naval base in the east of the island. However, in 1941, the RNEI Army decided against this. The manner of warfare in 1939 and 1940 in Europe led the RNEI Army command to conclude that 'rapid operations should be reckoned with, carried out in several places simultaneously, whereby one (or more) point(s) chosen by the opponent is being pushed through powerfully and quickly with the help of motorized and mechanized forces'. The Java Army therefore had to consist of rapidly deployable units in West, Central and East Java to execute quick, decisive counter-actions. This required extensive motorization and mechanization of the field army. Secondly, significant reinforcement of territorial forces on the coast and inland was deemed necessary for security.

The RNEI Army army command identified three key locations in the defence of Java:

1. The army and navy operating bases, namely Bandung and Surabaya;
2. The capital and seat of government Jakarta, and the port of Tanjung Priok;
3. Cilacap, the main port on the south coast.

The defence of Java was based on indirect coastal defence with direct coastal defence at the three main ports. The three key points were primarily defended by a direct coastal defence and by positions on the possible advance routes.

On the roads leading from West Java to Jakarta, on all access roads linking the Priangan Plateau with the city of Bandung, on the north–south roads in the narrow part of Java between Cirebon and Semarang and on the roads leading to Surabaya, anti-tank defensive positions were built suitable for an all-round defence. An extended position was constructed around Surabaya. Secondly, the mobile defence of the above-mentioned key points would be conducted by four regiments with auxiliary weapons. Relying on local defences, the mobile forces would operate as offensively as possible and defend the key points with counter-attacks against any enemy troops that landed.

After 1940, the system of direct coastal defence was expanded by adding artillery and coastal positions at the ports of Semarang, Pekalongan and Tegal. However, only limited resources could be made available for this.

On Java, it was also planned to execute guerrilla warfare after defeat in a conventional battle. However, few preparations were made for this.

# ALLIES

## Staff conferences 1940–41

As the threat from Japan increased, so did the Western Powers' need for mutual consultation. At the end of 1940 and 1941, this resulted in Anglo-Dutch, Anglo-American and Anglo-Dutch-Australian and multinational staff conferences in Singapore, Jakarta and Manila. These conferences were limited to military-level discussions. The United States was neutral and was unwilling or unable to make any concrete commitments. Great Britain and the Netherlands became allies in 1940, but Great Britain did not guarantee to come to the aid of the Netherlands East Indies in the event of a Japanese attack. The Netherlands itself followed a neutral course in Asia after 1940. All this explains why the Western Powers failed to reach a political agreement.

At the staff conferences, agreements were made to cooperate on a military operational level in the event of a Japanese attack. The Western Powers planned primary defensive operations in the Far East with a lack of maritime resources. Two simultaneous Japanese large-scale operations were considered unlikely. Four scenarios were identified for Japan. Under Scenario B, the British would receive military support from the Dutch following an attack on Malaya. The Dutch underlined the strategic importance of Singapore and made naval and air forces available for its defence. The Military Aviation Service would supply a group of three bomber squadrons (27 aircraft) and one fighter squadron, while the Royal Netherlands Navy made six to eight submarines available for this purpose. The Dutch surface fleet would be used for convoy protection to and from Singapore. It was agreed that, in order to deny the Japanese access to Borneo and the Netherlands East Indies, North Borneo, North Sulawesi and Ambon would be held. Against these Dutch commitments, Australia stated that they would supply an air strike force and army units for Ambon and Timor.

A joint and multinational headquarters was not set up. At most, liaison officers were exchanged. There was no question of large-scale multinational exercises.

## Unified Command (ABDACOM) 1942

Following the outbreak of war in the Pacific, the newly allied Prime Minister Winston Churchill and President Franklin D. Roosevelt met between 22

The first meeting of ABDACOM, 10 January 1942, in the official residence of the Dutch Commander of the Navy (*Commandant Zeemacht*) in Jakarta. At the head of the table is Colonel E.T. Kengen (Military Aviation Service). To the right of him are Lieutenant-Commander A.H.W. von Freytag Drabbe (RNN, standing), Group Captain L. Darvall (RAF), Major-General I.S. Playfair (Indian Army), Lieutenant-General Sir H.R. Pownall, General A.P. Wavell, Lieutenant-General G.H. Brett (USA), Major-General L.H. Brereton (USAAF), Air Commodore J.E. Hewitt (RAAF), Air Marshal Sir C.S. Burnett (RAAF), Rear Admiral J.J.A. van Staveren (RNN), Rear Admiral A.F. Palliser (RN), Vice Admiral Sir G. Layton (RN), Vice Admiral C.E.L. Helfrich (RNN), Admiral T.C. Hart (USN), Rear Admiral W.R. Purnell (USN), Lieutenant-General H. ter Poorten (RNEI Army) and Lieutenant-Colonel P.G. Mantel (RNEI Army). At this meeting, strategic and organizational decisions were taken. (Beeldbank WW2 – NIOD)

December 1941 and 14 January 1942 in Washington, DC at the Arcadia Conference. Here, fundamental agreements were reached about Allied warfare in Europe and Asia. The war goals were formulated in the Declaration of Nations. The heads of government further committed themselves to the 'Germany First' principle. Churchill and Roosevelt decided to establish a common Anglo-American military consultative body: the Combined Chiefs of Staff (CCS).

The Pacific was considered a secondary theatre. The principle there became 'hold territory'. The US Army Chief of Staff, General George C. Marshall, proposed unity of command in the South-West Pacific in the form of a joint, multinational (combined) headquarters. Given the vastness of the area of operations, the British doubted the effectiveness of such a headquarters. However, eventually they reluctantly agreed. British General Archibald P. Wavell was put forward by the Americans to be the Supreme Commander.

The joint and combined headquarters was named ABDA Command (ABDACOM), also known as Unified Command.[11] ABDACOM's mandate was to defend the Malay Barrier (Malaya, Sumatra, Java, northern Australia), retain Burma and Australia, restore communications with Luzon (the Philippines) through the Netherlands East Indies, support the garrison in the Philippines and maintain essential communication lines in the area.

ABDACOM formed an international chain of command on top of the already existing national service commands. ABDACOM was organized along British lines with headquarters for the multinational (combined) air forces, naval forces and land forces: ABDA-AIR, ABDA-FLOAT and ABDA-ARM. This meant that the RNEI Army and Royal Netherlands Navy were deprived of their air forces with their strategic reconnaissance capabilities. Instead, intelligence was centralized in the Combined Operations and Intelligence Centre (COIC). Due to the separate locations of the various land masses within the command, ABDA-ARM meant little. It was everyone for themselves.

ABDACOM did not actually control the Philippines. The Supreme Commander himself was focused on preserving Singapore. He had little regard for developments in the middle and eastern part of his area of authority.

---

11  ABDA stands for American-British-Dutch-Australian.

General A.P. Wavell on his arrival in Jakarta on 10 January 1942. On the left is the British Consul-General H.F.C. Walsh, while to the right (with back towards viewer) is Lieutenant-General H. ter Poorten and (facing the viewer) Admiral T.C. Hart (USN). Wavell was an experienced officer and commander, formerly the commander-in-chief Middle East Command and the current commander-in-chief India. As Supreme Commander ABDACOM, his decision-making was less fortunate. He used up scarce resources at Singapore, and sent in ground troops where air and naval reinforcements were needed. Because of his focus on Singapore, he hardly used any resources to counter the Japanese advance in the centre and east of the Indonesian archipelago. (Beeldbank WW2 – NIOD)

The Netherlands and Australia had been important partners during the staff conferences. This immediately ended with the outbreak of war in Asia. Strategic policy became an Anglo-American affair, with the Americans in the lead. The Dutch, Australian and also the New Zealand governments were deliberately not consulted and instead presented with a *fait accompli*. This not only applied to the institution, but also to appointments. British or American officers were appointed to all major command positions. Only ABDA-ARM was reserved for a Dutchman: the Army Commander H. ter Poorten. This clearly indicates the importance of that command. This state of affairs led to tensions with Australia and the Netherlands.

In early January 1942, upon British request, it was decided to move the Australian I Corps, consisting of the Australian 6th and 7th divisions, and the British 7th Armoured Brigade from the Middle East to the Netherlands East Indies. Wavell assigned a division to South Sumatra and a division along with the tank brigade to Central Java. With the fall of Singapore in sight, Wavell decided to divert these reinforcements to Burma. It was clear that with the fall of Singapore, the defence of India was his new priority. Australian political and military leadership no longer supported this British intention. Australian troops were needed in Australia. On 19 February 1942, the CCS decided to send no further land reinforcements to Java. Some Australian and British units, however, still disembarked there.

The question was whether the planned reinforcement of Java with ground troops could stop the Japanese advance – not to mention whether these would be operational in time. Given Japanese sea and airpower, a successful defence of the Netherlands East Indies was only possible with a large-scale reinforcement of Allied air and naval assets. However, sufficient aircraft were not available, while the Americans were unwilling to risk the US Pacific Fleet in the Western Pacific.

# Japanese Southern Offensive

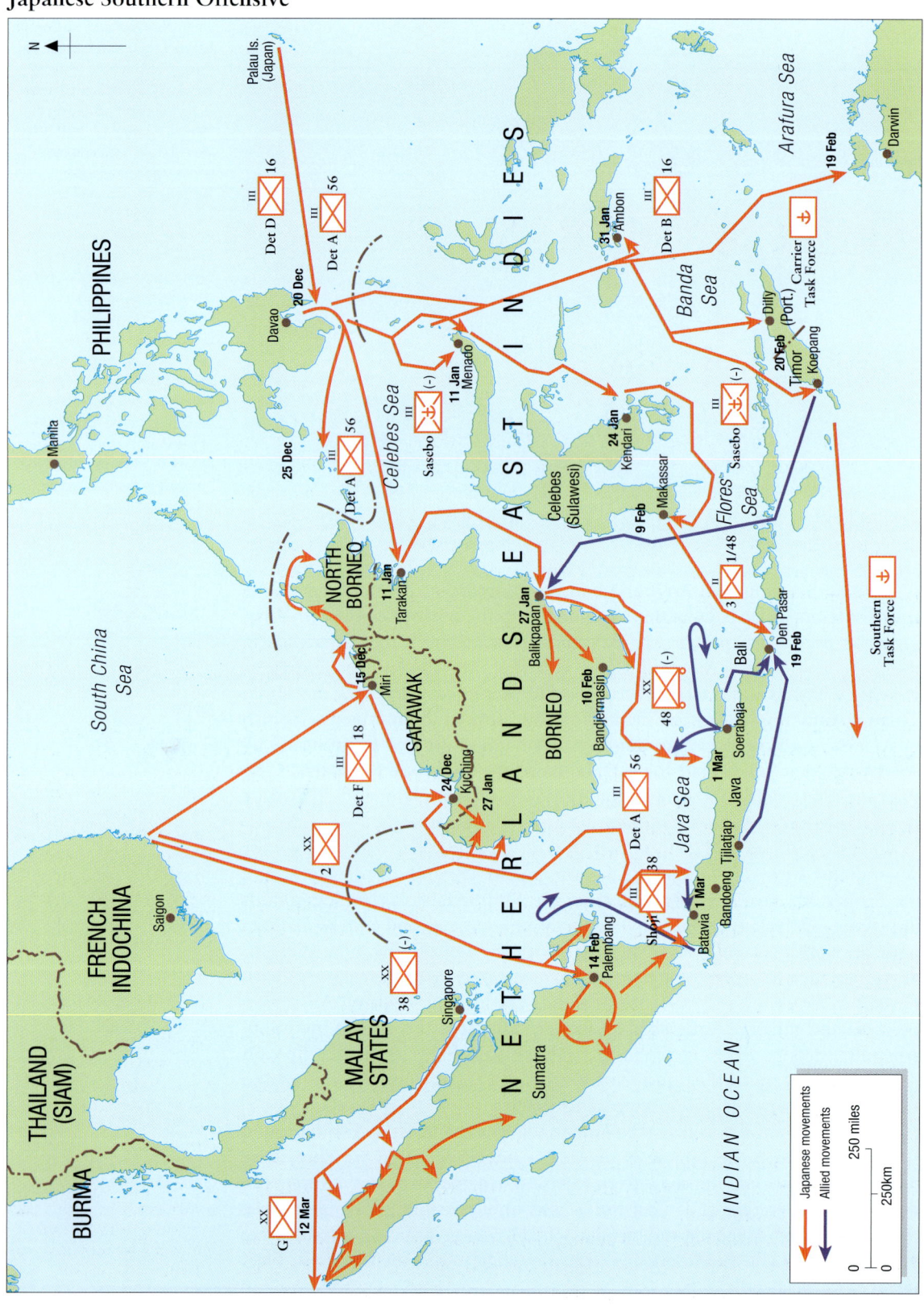

# THE CAMPAIGN

## PHASE I OPERATIONS

On 7/8 December 1941, Japan launched Operation *A-Go* with a simultaneous, broad-front offensive against assets of the United States and Great Britain. Although not directly attacked, the Netherlands declared war on Japan on 8 December 1941. In accordance with the agreements at the staff conferences, the NEI Military Aviation Service moved an aircraft group (wing) and a squadron of fighters to Malaya. The Royal Netherlands Navy dispatched a light cruiser and submarines. These units were placed under British operational command. In addition to the significant contribution of the Military Aviation Service and Royal Netherlands Navy, the RNEI Army sent four brigades (equivalent to sections) of the Marechaussee Corps, an infantry unit from Aceh specializing in anti-guerrilla operations. They were deployed behind the Japanese lines in Malaya in January and February 1942. Its strength was *c.* 142 men, including the Indonesian porters. After some successful actions, part of the detachment managed to return to Sumatra in March 1942.

After the Japanese landings in Siam and northern Malaya, shipping became available for Operation *B*: the conquest of British Borneo. Detachment F (Kawaguchi Detachment) landed from Indochina on 16 December 1941 at Miri and on 24 December 1941 at Kuching. The RNEI Army saw this as a serious threat and responded with bombing by the Military Aviation Service. The Royal Netherlands Navy deployed submarines against the Japanese amphibious operations at Kuching. These attacks inflicted considerable damage, but failed to halt the Japanese advance.

Davao, a port city on Mindanao in the Philippines, was occupied on 20 December 1941, with southern Jolo following suit on 25 December 1941. With the occupation of Kuching, Davao and Jolo, the bases for the attack on the Netherlands East Indies were in Japanese hands. Instead of the initially planned Palau, the geographically favourable and larger Davao became the assembly point for Operation *H*. While the operations against Malaya and the Philippines were still in full swing, the IJN switched to Phase II operations, the attack on the NEI, on 26 December 1941. The oil island of Tarakan off the coast of Borneo and Menado on North Sulawesi were the first targets to be attacked.

The state of the airfields at Kuching, Davao and Jolo turned out to be far worse than expected. The naval construction units needed more time to prepare these bases. Davao and Jolo were only fully available from 8

**OPPOSITE**
The Japanese Southern Offensive took place during the rainy season with a high-pressure system above the Asian mainland and the resulting North-East Monsoon in the Northern Hemisphere and the North-West Monsoon in the Southern Hemisphere. The wet monsoon brings moist air from the South China Sea and Pacific with heavy rain showers in the afternoon. Rain and poor visibility made air operations difficult. Atmospheric disturbances hindered flight movements and led to poor radio communications. The vegetation mostly consisted of tropical jungle. The few larger cities formed, as it were, islands in the jungle. The road network was limited in the extreme. Java was an exception. The main island was well connected with a modern road network and with rail and tramways.

**ABOVE LEFT**
From 1937, the RNEI Aviation Service reorganized the existing three reconnaissance and fighter aircraft squadrons into horizontal bomber squadrons. To this end, it purchased the American-built Glenn Martin B-10 Model 139 and Model 166 twin-engine bomber in 1936 and subsequent years. The aircraft in the photo are the WH-2 (Wright Holland-2) version with registration numbers M-514 and M-539. Three of the four crew members are visible. The aircraft bear the national markings introduced on 15 November 1939. Both aircraft were assigned to 2/3rd Aircraft Group in December 1941 and were lost at Sembawang (Singapore) or later at Kalidjati. (Museum Bronbeek)

**ABOVE RIGHT**
An Ambonese gunner with a magazine-fed 20mm Solothurn S18-1000 anti-tank rifle (*tankbuks* M38). In total, only 72 such rifles were available. The S18-1000 provided the infantry battalion with a portable anti-tank weapon. An anti-tank rifle group (ten men) with two anti-tank rifles was allocated to the 4th Company (heavy weapons) of each infantry battalion. (Beeldbank WW2 – NIOD)

January 1942. Despite these delays, the Japanese Southern Army wanted to bring forward the attack on Java by a month. It sought to capitalize on the favourable development of operations, maintain momentum and to be ahead of possible reinforcements of the US Navy and British Royal Navy. Given the delays in the commissioning of captured air bases, and the limited number of transport and naval escort ships available, the IJN argued against the bringing forward. Under great pressure from the IJA, the IJN finally agreed, in the Cam Ranh Agreement of 1 January 1942.

**Table 9: Operation *H* schedule: the Cam Ranh Agreement**

| Key area to capture | Tokyo Agreement (X day = start of the war) | Cam Ranh Agreement (X day = start of the war) |
| --- | --- | --- |
| Menado | X + 23 | X + 33 |
| Tarakan | X + 25 | X + 33 |
| Kendari | X + 35 | X + 43 |
| Balikpapan | X + 35 | X + 43 |
| Makassar | X + 45 | X + 53 |
| Bandjermasin | X + 50 | X + 53 |
| Ambon | X + 60 | X + 48 |
| Kupang | X + 60 | X + 65 |
| Bangka/Palembang | X + 80 | X + 60 |
| Java | X + 80 | X + 70 |
| Northern Sumatra | – | X + 80 |

The Allies recognized the importance of Davao and Jolo, and both locations were attacked from the air by Dutch and American units.

# PHASE II OPERATIONS: THE CONQUEST OF THE NEI

The Empire of Japan had on 8 December 1941 not declared war on the Netherlands. It was still attempting via Switzerland to bring the Netherlands East Indies peacefully within its sphere of influence as a protectorate, following the Indochina model. However, the Netherlands did not respond to this. Japan subsequently declared war on the Netherlands on 11 January 1942.

Operation *H*, the conquest of the NEI, was based on a rapid and methodical advance almost simultaneously over three axes towards the main island of Java: via South Sumatra from the west, through the Makassar Strait in the centre and via the Banda Sea from the east. The capture and preparation of air bases in South Sumatra, Borneo and Sulawesi was essential for the air operation against Java. Ambon and Kupang on Timor were to be occupied, to secure the left flank of the advance to Java and to sever Allied communcations with Australia.

# TARAKAN

At the end of December 1941, the IJN started the air campaign to eliminate Allied airpower on Tarakan and at Menado. On 4 January 1942, Tarakan Airfield was evacuated by the NEI Military Aviation Service. The Naval Aviation Service followed six days later. Without an early warning system and adequate ground-based air defence, the advanced airfield proved to be too vulnerable to air attacks. On 26 December 1941, an air strike followed on the Tondano naval air base, North Sulawesi. The naval air base was then closed down.

On 11 January 1942, the Japanese landed simultaneously on Tarakan and at Menado. The Sakaguchi Detachment and the 2nd Kure SLF attacked Tarakan. Tarakan was defended by the RNEI 7th Infantry Battalion, a field battalion with increased armament, and the 3rd Coastal and AA Artillery Company. The total strength of the garrison was 1,365 men. The commander, Lieutenant-Colonel S. de Waal, ordered the destruction of the oilfields and oiltank supplies on 10 January 1942.

The Japanese landed between midnight and 0430hrs at three points on the virtually undefended east coast.[12] The attack was delayed because the main force landed on the wrong beach. Thereafter, the infantry assault stalled due to Dutch resistance. A night attack managed to penetrate the defence. Two planned Dutch counter-attacks failed to materialize. The RNEI commander considered his defence to have been breached and had no reserves to plug the gap. The morning of the 12th, the garrison offered to surrender.

Unaware of the capitulation, the RNEI Karugan battery sank two Japanese minesweepers, the *W13* and *W14*, after the surrender; 159 sailors were killed. The IJN subsequently executed 215 prisoners of war from the battery on 19 January 1942. The Sakaguchi Detachment reported losses of seven killed and 35 injured. The 2nd Kure SLF reported three injured, and claimed to have killed some 300 soldiers of the RNEI Army, wounded 40 and taken 871 prisoner. According to Dutch reports, 33 soldiers died on Tarakan. This number does not include the military personnel executed on 19 January 1942.

Destroyed RNEI armoured cars on Tarakan. A mobile group of 80 men with seven APCs (*overvalwagen*) formed part of the garrison. The APCs were locally manufactured in Java by adding armour to a commercial truck chassis. One officer labelled the resultant APCs 'no good'. The armour needed to be resistant to small-arms fire. One vehicle commander reported, however, that he could see through the bullet holes in the armour after an engagement. The car was also difficult to turn on the road. The sign on the APC in this image is not Dutch, but the Japanese sign for an infantry brigade headquarters. To the right side of the road, alongside the APC, lie two dead NEI crew members. (Mainichi Newspapers)

The oil tank farm ablaze at Lingkas on Tarakan. Upon notification of the approach of the Japanese fleet, the destruction plan was put into effect in the afternoon and evening of 10 January 1942. The oil-drilling sites and the oil tank farm were destroyed. (Mainichi Newspapers)

# MENADO

On the morning of 11 January 1942, the Eastern Attack Unit with the Sasebo Combined SLF and the 1st Yokosuka SLF conducted an amphibious and airborne

---

12  All times are given in that of the relevant party. For the Japanese, this is Japan Standard Time (UTC + 09:00).

operation that caught the scattered NEI forces in a pincer movement from Menado in the west and Kema in the east, with Japanese paratroopers attacking in the centre by the Menado II Airfield (Langoan). Menado was defended by garrison troops of the Menado Troops Command, part of the Celebes and Menado Territorial Command, under Major B.F.A. Schilmöller. The strength was *c.* 1,500 men in a number of separate, unconnected units of widely differing combat value.

The coastal defence by the Menado Company was quickly overcome and the city was occupied. After a short but fierce battle, the paratroopers managed to capture the airfield. Two counter-attacks were launched by RNEI troops, but lacked coordination and were too weak. The paratroopers also captured the abandoned naval air base in the afternoon. The advance from Menado inland was held up by a delaying action. After this, RNEI coordinated resistance disintegrated.

The capture of Menado cost the Special Landing Forces 44 killed and 184 injured. Among the fallen were 12 paratroopers whose transport aircraft was shot down by their own fighter aircraft. Japan claimed 140 killed and 48 prisoners of war from the RNEI Army. According to Dutch records, 20 soldiers died, 11 of whom were executed.

The northern line of defence had been breached with the fall of Tarakan and Menado. For Wavell, with his emphasis on Singapore, the defence of bases in the northern and eastern periphery of the Netherlands East Indies was not a priority. He wanted to preserve his scarce air forces for the later battle. The Dutch and Americans clearly thought otherwise. Together, they deployed their airpower against the Japanese advance.

The Military Aviation Service and FEAF flew missions against the Japanese landing fleet at Tarakan and against its airfield. The latter was damaged, but overall the results were relatively limited. Japanese Zeke fighters inflicted a heavy toll. The Military Aviation Service lost a total of six bombers and 23 crew members. On 13 January 1942, the Military Aviation Service ended attacks on the island.

The Military Aviation Service lacked any means of attacking Menado, and so missions against the latter were flown by the RAAF and FEAF. The results were poor. The IJN spoke at Menado of 'fierce counter-attacks by enemy aircraft. It was fortunate that [the enemy] caused no [major] damage to us because their attacks were carried out by single planes, and, moreover, their skill was not very great. We observe that our losses must have been disastrous should we have been attacked by a considerable number of [enemy planes] in formation.'[13] Such an evaluation could apply equally to Tarakan.

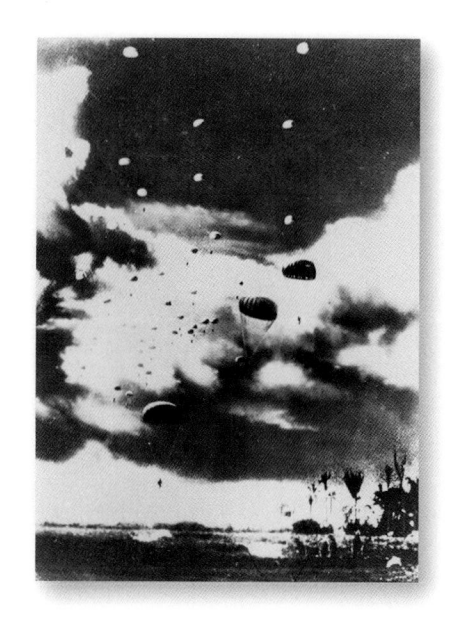

The assault by Japanese naval paratroopers on the Menado II Airfield (Lagoan) on Sulawesi was the first airborne operation in Asia. The 1st Yokosuka SLF jumped from 27 transport aircraft of the 1st Air Group. One aircraft was shot down by friendly fire. The weapons were to be dropped 150m after the personnel had jumped out. The only 37mm anti-tank gun was flown in by flying boat, landing on Lake Tondano. (Mainichi Newspapers)

# BALIKPAPAN

After two weeks, the Japanese made their second leap forward on 24 January 1942. Again, two amphibious operations were performed simultaneously. The Sakaguchi Detachment landed at Balikpapan, while the IJN attacked Kendari on Sulawesi.

13 Remmelink, W. (ed./trans.), *The Operations of the Navy in the Dutch East Indies and the Bay of Bengal*, The Corts Foundation/ Leiden University Press, 2018, pp. 167–71.

The preparation of Tarakan Airfield was seriously delayed. As a result, the IJA and IJN were not only forced to postpone the attack on Balikpapan for three days, but also to cancel the planned deployment of paratroopers. To take the oil installations (almost) intact, Sakaguchi sent two Dutch prisoners of war with an ultimatum to Balikpapan. Destruction of natural resources and facilities would be punished with death for the Dutch military. In addition, Sakaguchi adjusted the operation plan. Using surprise, a strong unit would infiltrate the hinterland via the river, and cut off the retreat route. The garrison would soon be forced to surrender. Two Indonesian police officers from Tarakan were said to have acted as guides. On 16 January 1942, nine Japanese fighters were stationed at Tarakan. Two days later, they began air strikes against Balikpapan.

Balikpapan was an important oil port in eastern Borneo, and contained an oil refinery with a large tank park (160 tanks). The city was located on a large bay surrounded by swamp and heavily overgrown hill country. The NEI garrison, numbering 1,200 men, consisted of the 6th Infantry Battalion, a field battalion (reduced) with two infantry companies and a machine-gun company, and the 2nd Coastal and AA Artillery Company. The garrison was ordered to defend Balikpapan against a *coup de main*, and to conduct a delaying action to gain time to carry out the destruction of the facilities. If Balikpapan fell into enemy hands, the order was to wage guerrilla war.

The commander of the NEI troops, Lieutenant-Colonel C. van den Hoogenband, did not respond to Sakaguchi's ultimatum and immediately began destroying the infrastructure. Once the oil facilities had been put out of use, the RNEI General Headquarters thought of withdrawing most of the garrison, chiefly to Bandjermasin. However, at the time of the Japanese landing, a decision was yet to be made.

The Sakaguchi Detachment landed at 0240hrs on 24 January 1942 at three locations outside the defended coastal areas. The destroyed and vacated Manggar Airfield and the Samboja drilling site were captured without resistance. The advance towards the city was severely affected by road demolitions. The landing in the bay north of the city threatened the garrison in the rear. Given the progress in destroying the oil infrastucture and the threat of being cut off, Van den Hoogenband decided not to defend Balikpapan. He broke off the fight and retreated inland with 700 men. In view of the destruction carried out, Sakaguchi fulfilled his threat. On 20 February 1942, 78 civilians and prisoners of war were executed on the beach.

**ABOVE LEFT**
The Menado II Airfield (Lagoan) under airborne attack by the 1st Yokosuka SLF. The Japanese paratroopers jumped directly onto the target from an altitude of 150m. The airfield was still under construction, but the runway could support fighter aircraft. The Japanese put the airfield into operation immediately. On 16 January 1942, the HQ of the 21st Air Flotilla moved in from Davao. (Mainichi Newspapers)

**ABOVE RIGHT**
A light machine-gun section of the 1st Yokosuka SLF led by an officer, in position at Menado II Airfield (Langoan). The group weapon is a Type 96 (1936) 6.5mm Nambu light machine gun. The machine gunner wears the trade badge of seaman 2nd class. (Public domain)

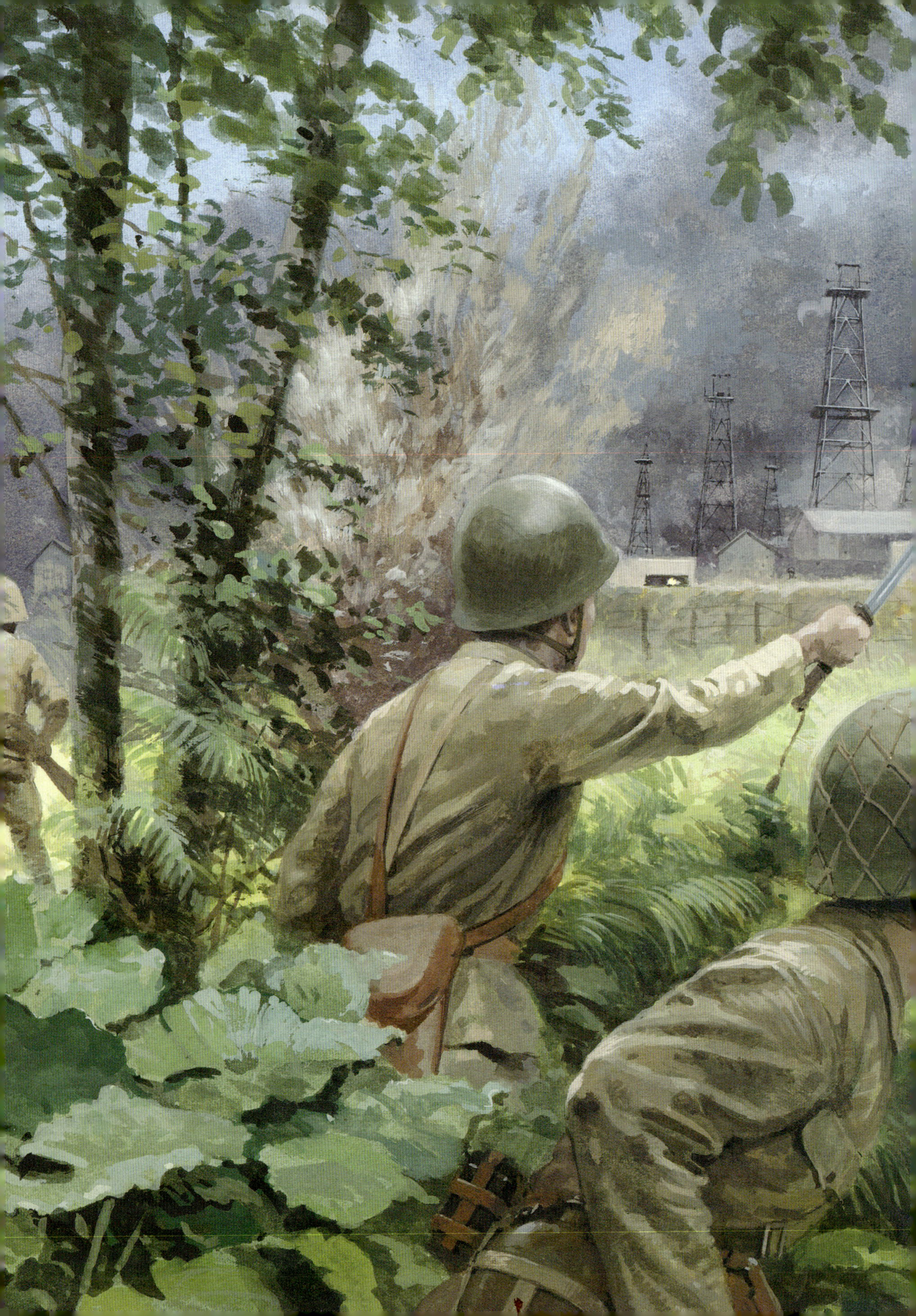

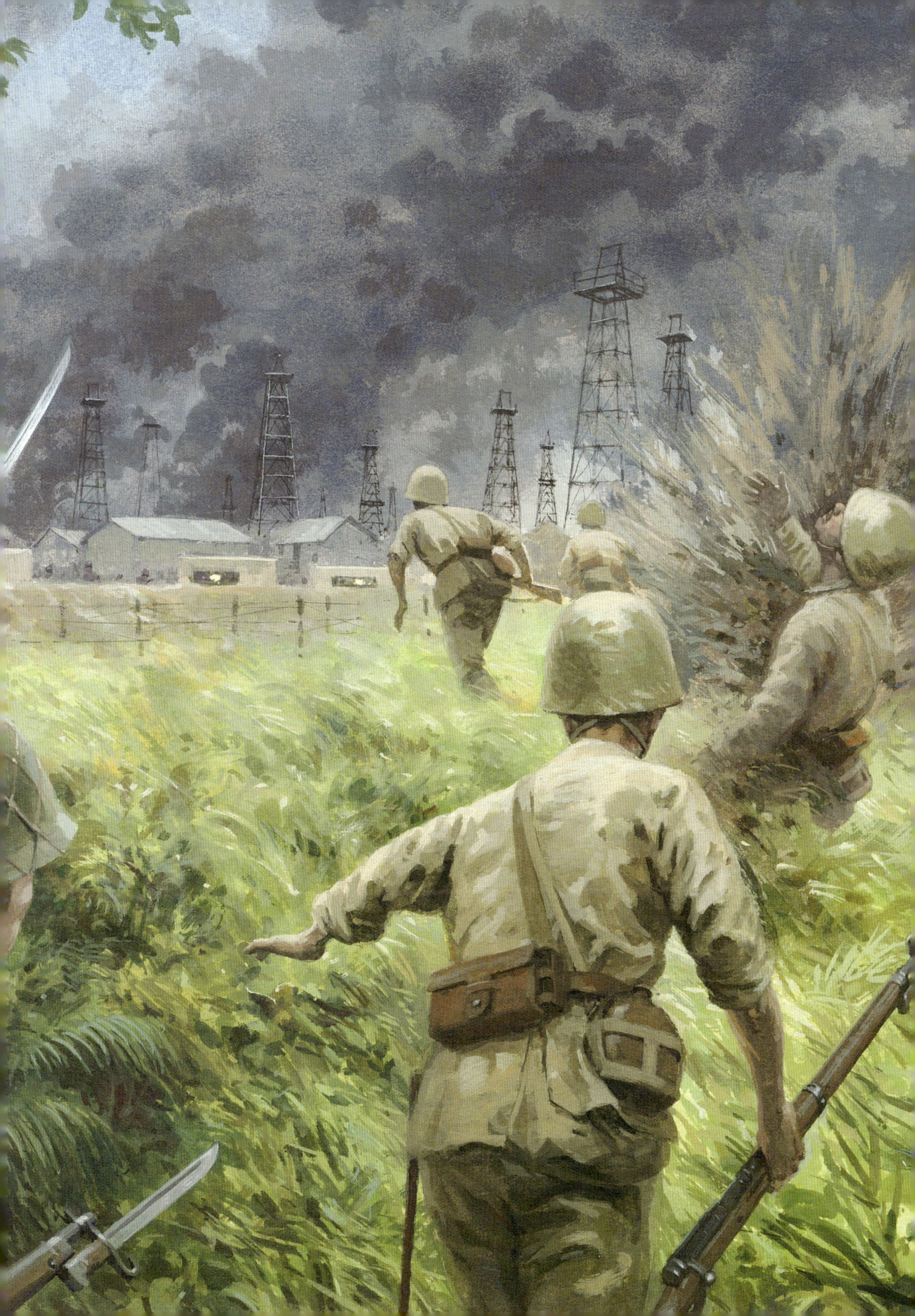

**ATTACK ON NEI STRONGPOINT NO.10, EASTERN FRONT, TARAKAN, 11 JANUARY 1942 (PP. 42–43)**

On 11 January 1942, the Sakaguchi Detachment and the 2nd Kure SLF began their amphibious attack on Tarakan at three points on the east coast. The Right Wing Unit – comprising 1st Battalion and two companies from 3rd Battalion, 146th Infantry Regiment, half the regimental artillery and 1st Engineer Company (reduced) – and the 2nd Kure SLF landed at 0000hrs and 0030 hrs (JST). According to the plan, the drilling site (in the centre of the island), Lingkas and the Karungan batteries (on the west coast) would be in Japanese hands by dawn. The airfield would then be captured.

From the start, the operation did not go according to plan. The Right Wing Unit landed 4–6km north of the planned landing point, delaying the start of the attack considerably, and surprise was lost. Then the Left Wing Unit became disoriented in the dense jungle and did not reach, let alone capture, their objective of the Karungan batteries.

The Right Wing Unit marched through flooded forests to reach the intended landing point, and then, at daybreak, they stormed and overwhelmed the NEI strongpoint at Amal. The attack on the NEI Eastern Front began around 0930hrs local time. The Eastern Front consisted of five mutually supporting strongpoints, numbered 8 to 12. Only strongpoints 10 and 11 were occupied by the NEI defenders, which weakened the firing line. These strongpoints lay directly on the Japanese axis of advance.

Here we see the Japanese infantry attack on Strongpoint No. 10 (**1**). In the background oil-drilling towers (**2**) can be seen. Strongpoint 10 was under the command of Sergeant Terbrugge, while No. 11 was manned by 1st Lieutenant J.C. den Hond, his staff, a section of MMGs and two LMG groups (totalling 23 men). Each strongpoint consisted of six concrete pillboxes (**3**): one command post with observation post, four pillboxes for the MGs and a reserve position for one of the automatic weapons in the rear. Each pillbox had room for two men. The other troops (ammunition handlers) were located in trenches protected by an earth rampart. The MMG provided flanking fire. The two LMGs gave frontal protection. The strongpoints were protected by a double barbed-wire obstacle (**4**) approximately 30m in front of the pillboxes. The whole position was protected by a double wire obstacle 40–50m to its front. All obstacles were covered by flanking fire from the MGs. The fields of fire were hindered by the fast-growing tropical vegetation (**5**). The Japanese advance was halted by mortar and 7.5cm artillery fire (**6**), and intense NEI small-arms fire. Around 1000hrs, Strongpoint 10 was finally captured after Sergeant Terbrugge was killed and the rest of the defenders withdrew.

The NEI commander, Lieutenant-Colonel De Waal, had established a second defensive line manned by improvised units and held the Ambonese 1st Company, 7th Infantry Battalion from the Linkasfront in reserve. However, when ordered to counter-attack, the company refused to move forward under fire.

The Japanese planned to break the defences using a night attack. They managed to penetrate the NEI positions and even occupy the two Dutch barracks, but the second NEI line held. IJN air support was called in to bomb the NEI batteries in the morning. Lieutenant-Colonel De Waal ordered a second Dutch counter-attack in the morning to reestablish the front line. In the chaos following the Japanese night attack, however, the assigned troops instead withdrew to the airfield. De Waal now considered his line breached, and he had no reserves to plug the gap. That same morning, the NEI troops surrendered.

The losses among Sakaguchi's force amounted to eight casualties on land and 39 at sea.

ABDACOM became operational on 15 January 1942, and was now facing its first test. It deployed air and naval forces against the Japanese landing fleet heading for Balikpapan. The Military Aviation Service flew missions against the Japanese ships. From Java, FEAF conducted several missions in January. Air strikes caused the Japanese landing fleet to lose two transport ships and damaged three transport ships, a seaplane tender and a destroyer. The Japanese convoy had already been attacked en route on 23 January 1942 by Dutch submarines; a transport ship was sunk. Shortly after the landing boats departed, the anchored Japanese transport ships were unexpectedly attacked by the four American destroyers of Destroyer Division 59 at around 0300hrs. In a 'hit-and-run' attack, these ageing warships sank four transport ships, damaging two others and a patrol boat. At least 121 Japanese sailors lost their lives. Despite a massive Japanese air and naval presence, the Allies had inflicted significant losses on the Japanese transport fleet heading for Balikpapan.

On 23 January 1942, the Japanese discovered the secret airfield Samarinda II using air reconnaissance. After several air attacks, the remaining Military Aviation Service aircraft were withdrawn from Samarinda II. The base remained operational for the time being. The Military Aviation Service command decided to use Oelin Airfield at Bandjermasin for hit-and-run attacks from Java on Balikpapan. On 27 January 1942, a squadron was surprised on the ground by an air raid and was destroyed. In total, nine Glenn Martins were lost in this attack. This marked the end of any deployment by the Military Aviation Service above Borneo.

At Balikpapan there was an oil refinery with an oil tank farm to process and store oil from the drilling sites at Sambodja and Sanga-Sanga. On 20 January 1942, the RNEI Army troop commander opted to destroy the oil facilities and Manggar Airfield. Over the following days, a thick smokescreen hung over the city and the bay, causing black rain. Against this apocalyptic background, here we see five soldiers of the Sakaguchi Detachment advancing after their landing on 24 January 1941. (Mainichi Newspapers)

# KENDARI

Simultaneously with the attack on Balikpapan, the Eastern Attack Unit based on Menado struck the important Kendari II Airfield in South-East Sulawesi. Here, too, the landing by the Sasebo Combined SLF took place in the early morning (0422hrs). The same day, the city and (at 1700hrs) the airfield were occupied almost undamaged. The RNEI Army garrison at Kendari had about 500 men. The planned robust defence of the airfield did not take place due to weak leadership and a resultant lack of willingness to fight. The NEI troops withdrew to the interior, where a large part deserted or were even sent on leave. At least six NEI soldiers were killed on 24 January 1942.

The IJN switched to Phase III operations on 24 January 1942. With the conquest of Balikpapan and Kendari, Java came within flying range of the Japanese land-based bombers and fighters.

# SINGKAWANG

Because Kuching Airfield did not meet Japanese expectations, the IJN put its hopes on the secret airfield discovered on 20 December 1941, Singkawang II

# THE JAPANESE ASSAULT ON MENADO, 11–12 JANUARY 1942

The Japanese captured Menado Langoan (II) airfield and the seaplane base with a simultaneous amphibious and airborne assault by naval landing and airborne forces. The NEI forces were caught in a pincer movement, from Menado in the west and Kema in the east, with Japanese paratroopers attacking in the centre near the airfield. The scattered and outnumbered NEI forces managed to slow the inland advance of the Japanese amphibious forces by delaying actions from prepared positions. They could not, however, prevent them from establishing overland contact with the paratroopers. The airfield was fiercely defended, but fell into Japanese hands after a brief fight. NEI counter-attacks lacked coordination, were too weak, and failed, whereupon remnants of the garrison retreated into the mountains to begin an ill-fated guerrilla campaign.

## ▼ EVENTS

Times are given in Japan Standard Time (JST – UTC+09:00) unless otherwise stated. Celebes Time (CBT) was UTC+08:00.

**11 January 1942**

1. 0400hrs: Amphibious night landing of Sasebo Combined SLF HQ with support units and 1st Sasebo SLF (c. 1,800 men) north and south of Menado. The outnumbered NEI defenders are caught off-guard and soon cut off. The Japanese seize the city at 0830hrs.

2. 0420hrs: Amphibious night landing of 2nd Sasebo SLF (c. 1,400 men) at Kema. The small NEI coastal guard detachment (two sections) of A Company is driven off. The Japanese force moves inland by road, spearheaded by three light tanks.

3. 0952–1020hrs: First drop of 1st Yokosuka SLF consisting of battalion HQ, signal unit and 1st and 2nd companies (334 men) at Langoan Airfield. The NEI defenders lay down heavy cross-fire, but are forced to retreat. By 1125hrs, the airfield is in Japanese hands.

4. 0945hrs: 1st Sasebo SLF, spearheaded by four light tanks, heads for Tomohon, but is slowed by successful NEI delaying actions using the prepared defensive position at Tinoör and an ambush at Kakaskasen. The numerically superior Japanese push forward and seize Tomohon at 1930hrs.

5. To block the route from Kema inland, A Company issues orders to concentrate at Ajermadidih. Only one section (20 men), reinforced with a section from Menado Company, manages to reach the prepared position to fight a delaying action around 1300hrs. The 2nd Sasebo SLF occupies Ajermadidih at 1400hrs.

6. At Kakas, the Mobile Column (two armoured cars) is sent to support the airfield defenders. It runs into a Japanese reconnaissance squad. Only the crew of one armoured car manages to reach Kakas, on foot, in a fighting retreat.

7. During the morning, the Officer Commanding Menado moves most of his reserves from Kakas to stop the Japanese advance inland. A counter-attack by the two remaining sections of KV Company in the direction of the airfield from the south fails.

8. 1300hrs: Having secured the airfield, 1st Yokosuka SLF heads towards the secondary objective of Tasoeka seaplane base. C Company (reduced), west of Kakas, fails to block the Japanese advance. At 1450hrs, Kakas is taken followed at 1800hrs by the seaplane base. The main body of 1st Yokosuka SLF returns to the airfield.

9. 1450hrs: Two Japanese flying boats, carrying the 1st Yokosuka SLF's paymaster, medical and AT units, land on Lake Tondano.

**12 January 1942**

10. In the morning, the Japanese 3rd Company jumps onto Langoan Airfield. The 1st Yokosuka SLF then launches a full-scale attack on Langoan city; it is taken at 1125hrs, followed by Tompaso at 1230hrs. Paso is seized at 1100hrs.

11. 0810hrs: Sasebo Combined SLF captures Tondano. The 1st Sasebo SLF heads for the airfield along the road from Tomohon to Tompaso. The 2nd Sasebo SLF moves by road along the western and eastern shores of the lake.

12. 1100hrs: 2nd Sasebo SLF makes contact with 1st Yokosuka SLF near Paso. 1st Sasebo SLF establishes contact at 1230hrs near Tompaso. They reach Langoan and Kakas by 1400hrs. The operation is over.

**12 January–20 February 1942**

13. Remnants of the NEI garrison begin a planned-for guerrilla war, but the lack of popular support and resources, and the unsuitable terrain, dooms it to failure. After the fall of the major towns, desertion is high in almost all the remaining NEI units. By the end of February, all is over.

## JAPANESE
**Sasebo Combined Special Landing Force:**
- **A.** 1st Sasebo SLF
- **B.** 2nd Sasebo SLF
- **C.** 1st Yokosuka SLF

MORI

MAPANGET AIRFIELD
MAPANGET
MENADO
AJERMADIDIH
KEMA
NDANO

TC — Menado
SCHILMÖLLER

## NEI
**Menado Troops Command**
1. Menado Company and two 7.5cm guns
2. A Company, Veteran Reserve Corps
3. Detachment E, Veteran Reserve Corps (45 men); coastal guard stationed on the west coast (beyond map confines)
4. European Militia and Homeguard Company
5. Menadonese Militia Company (beyond map confines, took no part in the fighting)
6. Town Guard

Kakas Tactical Command:
7. C Company, Veteran Reserve Corps, and three 3.7cm guns on trucks
8. D Company, Veteran Reserve Corps
9. Mobile Column (45 men in three armoured cars)

Reserve:
10. KV Company (Short Service)
11. B Company, Veteran Reserve Corps

Note: gridlines are shown at intervals of 5km (3.1 miles)

*Kendari II Airfield on Sulawesi was described as one of the best airfields in the Indonesian archipelago; it had three runways (1,000m by 600m), and was easy to extend. Unlike most other captured airfields, it could be put into use immediately. One drawback was that the airfield was far from the coast, lying 25km inland. On 27 February 1942, the 21st Air Flotilla HQ moved from Menado to the airfield. Kendari provided the Japanese with an important base for operations against Ambon and Timor, and thus against the Java–Australia line of communication. This picture was taken in 1947. (Leiden University Libraries, CC BY 4.0)*

(referred to as Ledo in Japanese sources). On 28 December 1941, the Southern Army ordered the Kawaguchi Detachment to prepare for the capture of this base. To the chagrin of the Southern Army, however, Kawaguchi saw little point in an operation against Singkawang II. On 6 January 1942, the annoyed leadership of Southern Army ordered Kawaguchi to conquer Singkawang as soon as possible.

By the end of January 1942, the Kawaguchi Detachment had begun a large pincer movement. Overland, a force moved towards Singkawang and captured the thoroughly destroyed airfield on 27 January 1942. A second force moved in improvised sea transport and landed successively in four locations along the west coast. The RNEI West Borneo Garrison Battalion, with a strength of approximately 1,000 men and already compromised morale, was tasked with the defence of West Borneo. It was reinforced with the 2nd Battalion, 15th Punjab Regiment of the British Indian Army, that had been withdrawn from Kuching with a remaining strength of 783 men. This force could only slow the Japanese advance. After the general capitulation in March 1942, the remaining NEI troops surrendered. A few continued to conduct guerrilla warfare. The 2nd Battalion, 15th Punjab Regiment withdrew to South Borneo, and then surrendered on 31 March. Japanese losses were 19 men killed, two fatally injured and 31 wounded in action. They reported 270 enemy killed and 182 prisoners of war taken.

Due to the destruction, the wet ground and the long-destroyed supply route over land, Singkawang II could not be used for the landing operation on Java. The IJN 22nd Air Flotilla therefore transferred its headquarters to Kuching on 8 February 1942. Due to the poor conditions at Kuching, aircraft could not be fuelled with a full load. This made carrying out air strikes on Java difficult.

With the loss of Singkawang II, Manggar at Balikpapan, Kendari II and the elimination of Samarinda II, the second line of strategic airfields had been broken.

# AMBON

Ambon is an irregularly shaped island with a long coastline and a small surface of 716km$^2$. It consists of two land masses, Hitu and Laitimor, separated by a large inner bay. It has low and medium mountains with peaks rising to between 460m and 1,000m. These are very steep and densely covered with secondary forest. There are few roads outside built-up areas, only animal trails and footpaths.

After 1936, the island of Ambon was developed into an auxiliary support base for the Royal Netherlands Navy. The island was centrally located in the eastern part of the Indonesian archipelago. The inner bay provided a sheltered natural harbour. It had two air bases: Halong Naval Air Base and Laha Airfield with a 1,700m-long concrete runway.

The garrison consisted of the Moluccas Garrison Battalion and the 4th Coastal and AA Artillery Company. The Garrison Battalion was made up of a headquarters, three companies, a machine-gun company, a *kortverband* (short service) company, a (European) militia company, a Veteran Reserve

Corps and detachments outside Ambon. In addition, four APCs were also sent to Ambon. The garrison also featured the Indonesian Militia Depot Battalion and Town and Country Guards. In total, it was about 2,600 men strong. In addition to these ground troops, the Military Aviation Service stationed a patrol of three fighter aircraft on Laha. The Royal Netherlands Navy stationed a squadron of seaplanes on Ambon.

To bolster the defence of Laha, the Australian Gull Force arrived on 17 December 1941, consisting of HQ Gull Force; the reinforced 2/21st Battalion; C Troop, 18th Anti-Tank Battery; a section of engineers from 2/11th Field Company; and some support elements, with a total strength of *c.* 1,170 men. An Area Combined Headquarters was established for the command of RNEI and Australian forces. On Laha, Gull Force suffered particularly from malaria and dysentery. Two weeks prior to the Japanese landing, the commanding officer Gull Force was replaced with Lieutenant-Colonel W.J.R. Scott. The collaboration between the latter and the NEI territorial commander left much to be desired.

The IJN wanted to sever the Allied Ambon–Kupang line of communication. As part of the elimination of Allied airpower in preparation for the attack on Menado, the IJN 21st Air Flotilla bombed Ambon. This was the beginning of a series of air strikes, followed by armed reconnaissance. Shortly before the landings, new air raids followed, this time by carrier-based aircraft. Under Japanese pressure and the now-reconnoitered invasion fleet, ABDACOM ordered the withdrawal of the remaining air units on 27 January 1942.

The NEI territorial commander, Lieutenant-Colonel J.L.R. Kapitz, followed a plan based on the fixed defence of coastal positions by the NEI troops, the defence of Laha Airfield by part of Gull Force and the formation of a covering force or general reserve by the rest of Gull Force and part of the NEI troops. On 10 January 1942, as proposed by Kapitz, it was decided that Gull Force would defend the southern part of Laitimor alongside Laha. Landings on the south-east coast of Laitimor were not expected. The mountain paths inland of the south-east coast were defended by three positions manned with semi-trained Indonesian militia sections. In view of the terrain, the NEI–Australian plan was mainly defensive in nature.

When it became clear on 30 January 1942 that the Japanese would land in the south, Kapitz expected it to take place at Passo. He therefore moved the centre of gravity of the defence to the Passo position: three companies, the machine-gun company and a militia section. This position was north of Ambon City on the isthmus between Hitu and Laitimor. With this, Kapitz increased the distance from Gull Force in the south. The Allied forces were further fragmented by this, and could be defeated piecemeal by an already powerful opponent.

The Eastern Attack Unit and the Air Task Force of the Southern Task Force carried out the attack on Ambon. The 2nd Carrier Division was placed under the command of the Air Unit. It was a considerable force. Between 0240 and 0250hrs on Saturday, 31 January 1942, Japan's Eastern Detachment (Ito Detachment), consisting of the 228th Infantry Regiment, 38th Division, landed from Hong Kong via Davao on two beaches on the undefended southeast coast of Ambon. This threatened the rear of the heavily fortified bay at Ambon. After the successful landing, the left attack unit, the main force, crossed the mountain ridge in two parallel columns over jungle trails under heavy rainfall and a stormy westerly wind (Beaufort Force 8). The weather

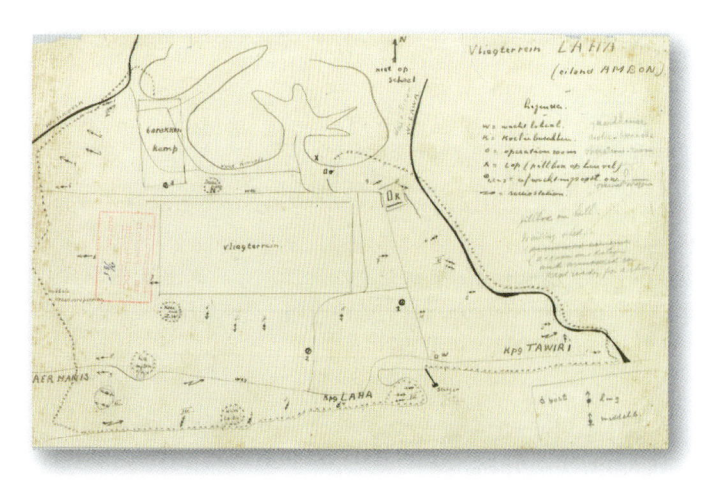

A sketch of the defence of Laha Airfield, located on a coastal plain at the inner bay of the island of Ambon. It was one of the few airfields in the Netherlands East Indies with a concrete runway. Quarters, stores and shelters were not dispersed or camouflaged, and were in the immediate vicinity of the airfield, which made the airfield particularly vulnerable – the more so because the ground-based air defence was weak, with two 4cm AA guns and three M.30 (Colt-Browning) 12.7mm AA guns from the RNEI Army. (Netherlands Institute of Military History)

cleared around noon. The reinforced NEI defenders were pushed aside. In the afternoon, the Japanese entered Ambon City. The RNEI Army and Australian troops were thus separated.

The Passo position was a prepared but not yet fully finished position facing north-east. The position was attacked by the right attack unit, the 2nd Battalion (reduced) of the 228th Infantry Regiment, from the south-east. Once again, the Japanese surprised the defenders. This attack was carried out during poor weather and brought the Japanese deep into the rear of the position around 1000hrs. An uncoordinated counter-attack soon stalled under Japanese fire. With that, the Passo position fell. That evening, Kapitz decided to surrender.

The 1st Kure SLF (750 men) reinforced with the 10th Company, 3rd Battalion, 228th Infantry Regiment arrived from Menado and performed an amphibious landing near Hitulama at 0200hrs, aiming for Laha Airfield. For more than an hour, the landing was contested by an infantry section from 4th Company of the Garrison Battalion reinforced with machine guns and mortars in pillboxes. Afterwards, the Japanese advance inland was slowed by a delaying action of the retreating NEI troops, the very poor weather and the bad state of the road network. Arriving at the inner bay, the SLF also took artillery fire from the NEI batteries on the other side. An initial attack on the airfield by the end of the afternoon stalled in gunfire and mortar fire from the defending Australians of B and C companies, 2/21st Battalion. Support was given by artillery fire from the Nona battery. The IJA 10th Company was sent into the jungle to conduct an envelopment. Furthermore, air support was received. Two further attacks on consecutive nights failed. On the morning of 3 February 1942, the Japanese attackers managed to penetrate the Allied positions. That morning, the 10th Company attacked the defenders in their rear after a difficult trek through the jungle. Laha capitulated.

Major-General Takeo Ito expected to capture the south of Laitimor the same day that Kapitz surrendered, 1 February 1942. The left attack unit turned south that day with two battalions abreast. South of Ambon City, the rest of Gull Force had dug in: A and D companies, 2/21st Battalion and most of the support units, with their improvised positions not facing the coast as expected, but north. At the urgent request of Scott, he was reinforced on 31 January 1942 with the NEI 2nd Company, Garrison Battalion. The Japanese gradually drove the Australian and NEI troops back under cover of artillery and mortar fire. In the morning of 3 February 1942, surrender and captivity followed for the Allied defenders.

The Eastern Detachment had suffered 55 killed and 135 injured, and the 1st Kure SLF 40 killed and 50 seriously injured. The Japanese claimed 340 Allied soldiers killed and 2,182 taken prisoner (782 Australians, 334 Dutch and 1,066 Indonesian troops). According to Australian reports, 49 Australian soldiers lost their lives. On 6, 15 and 20 February 1942, the majority of Australian prisoners of war taken at Laha were executed by the IJN.

# MAKASSAR

The Japanese wanted to take Makassar on Sulawesi and establish it as a base for the air offensive against Java. The operation was purely a naval affair of the Netherlands East Indies Unit and was carried out by the 1st Base Unit with air support from the 2nd Air Unit. Given the activities of the Allies in the Makassar Strait, this attack was not carried out from Menado around the west of Sulawesi, but via Kendari around the east and south of Sulawesi. An additional advantage of this clockwise operation was the possibility of assigning units from the Ambon operation. The attack was scheduled for 9 February 1942. The amphibious landing was to be conducted by the Sasebo Combined SLF.

In addition to the Celebes and Menado Territorial Command, Makassar also housed the Makassar Troops Command. Colonel M. Vooren was in command of all troops on Sulawesi, but he lacked the means to control the scattered detachments after the Japanese landings. The Makassar Troops Command consisted of *c.* 1,000 men of the Celebes and Menado Garrison Battalion. Colonel Vooren based his defence concept on the Malaya campaign. He set the goal of inflicting as greater losses as possible and tying down enemy units for as long as could be achieved. To this end, he traded the generally followed operational concept of direct coastal defence for an indirect defence: slowing down the enemy advance to carry out the planned destruction of Mandai Airfield, and ending in the defence of the Tjamba position in the mountainous interior. The entire plan was defensive.

The Japanese naval convoy was attacked by submarines. Although one Japanese destroyer was damaged and one was sunk, this did not hinder the amphibious landing. At around midnight Sunday 8–Monday 9 February 1942, the Sasebo Combined SLF made an amphibious landing in two areas 3km south of Makassar. The city was occupied around noon. The NEI defenders succeeded in destroying Mandai Airfield. At the end of the day, the offensive phase of the operation had ended for the IJN, leaving only mopping-up operations. The IJN claimed to have killed 77 enemy troops and taken 85 prisoners of war. Japanese losses were four killed in action and five injured from the SLF, and five killed and six seriously injured on board the sunken destroyer.

The NEI garrison had fallen back on the Tjamba position. The latter was only attacked on 27 February 1942, and taken the following day. The remaining RNEI Army troops melted away through desertion. In addition, the population had openly adopted an anti-Dutch attitude. On 7 March 1942, the NEI territorial commander surrendered. Little had come of his goal of tying down the Japanese.

# BANDJERMASIN

At a conference in Manila held between 21 and 23 January 1942, the IJN proposed extending the operating schedule by ten days and dropping the planned conquest of Bandjermasin. Preparing the airfield would probably take some time. Given the proximity to Java, supplying it was a major risk. Instead, it would be more effective in terms of risks to take Bali. However, the IJA adhered to the Cam Ranh Agreement. The capture of Bandjermasin was

# THE JAPANESE ASSAULT ON AMBON, 31 JANUARY–3 FEBRUARY 1942

The island of Ambon was centrally located in the eastern part of the Indonesian archipelago. It had a natural harbour and a well-equipped airport. The Japanese attack on the island comprised a joint army and naval amphibious assault at two separate landing zones, culminating in two separate operations: one on the southern peninsula by the IJA against the rapidly defeated NEI troops and the more resilient Australian Gull Force; and the other by the IJN on the northern peninsula, which attacked and ultimately took Laha Airfield.

## ▼ EVENTS

Times are given in Japan Standard Time (JST – UTC+09:00) unless otherwise stated. Moluccas Time (MCT) was UTC+08:30.

### Saturday, 31 January 1942

1. 0240hrs and 0250hrs: Unopposed amphibious night landing of Eastern Detachment on the south-east coast of Laitimor. The right attack unit marches towards Passo, the left via two steep mountain tracks towards Ambon City in poor weather.

2. The NEI militia platoons at Rutung and Sojadiattas delay the Japanese western attack.

3. 0100hrs: Amphibious night landing by the reinforced 1st Kure SLF (c. 1,000 men) at Hitoelama. NEI platoon from 4th Company, Garrison Battalion (reinforced) offers stiff resistance from prepared positions.

4. 0320hrs: NEI opposition at Hitoelama is overrun and the landing completed. The NEI detachment withdraws and conducts delaying actions on the route of advance.

5. c. 0800hrs (MCT): NEI reinforcements are sent piecemeal to the Rutung and Sojadiattas mountain detachments. They run into the two advancing Japanese left-attack columns and are mostly scattered. Lieutenant-Colonel Kapitz has expended his reserves.

6. 0730 hrs (MCT): The Japanese right attack assaults the Passo position in the right flank, overruns the flanking position at Batoegong and occupies the eastern strongpoints. 0830hrs (MCT) and 0930hrs (MCT): Two successive counter-attacks make almost no headway, and the Passo position is almost taken.

7. Advancing along poor roads in heavy rain, the 1st Kure SLF comes under heavy artillery fire from NEI coastal batteries on the opposite shore. The late-afternoon assault on Laha Airfield by the 2nd Company, 1st Kure SLF and 10th Company, 3rd Battalion, 228th Infantry Regiment is repulsed.

8. 1700hrs: The Japanese left attack unit enters Ambon City.

9. The 10th Company, 3rd Battalion, 228th Infantry Regiment is sent into the jungle to envelop the airfield from the high ground to the north.

### Sunday, 1 February 1942

10. 0130hrs: Lieutenant-Colonel Kapitz and the NEI troops in the Passo position surrender.

11. 1100hrs: The Japanese left attack pushes south from Ambon City. Gull Force has improvised a defence in depth to the south-west, but during the day the position is surrounded.

12. The Australian second line at Amahoesoe comes under attack. This position is defended by the Battalion HQ, D Company of 2/21st Battalion and service and support units Gull Force.

### Night, 1/2 February 1942

13. 2200hrs: Japanese 2nd Company manages to penetrate the eastern position between B and C companies, 2/21st Battalion, but the line holds and the Japanese attackers are pinned down.

14. Lieutenant-Colonel Scott, CO Gull Force, incorrectly believes Mt Nona has been occupied by the Japanese. He orders a withdrawal from the Amahoesoe line to Eri.

### Monday, 2 February 1942

15. 1200hrs: The Japanese attack on Laha is called off and air stikes and naval gunfire support are called in, and reinforcements requested.

16. 0630hrs: The Eastern Detachment occupies Mt Nona (Hill 514).

17. Morning: The 21st Minesweeper Division covered by the 15th Destroyer Division starts to clear the outer bay of mines. Minesweepers No. 11 and No. 12 strike mines and are badly damaged, and No. 9 sinks.

### Tuesday, 3 February 1942

18. 0115hrs: A second night assault takes place by the entire 1st Kure SLF on Laha, and breaks through the Australian defences. At 0615hrs, the airfield is captured. IJA reinforcements arrive after the Australian surrender.

19. Under shelling and bombardment, and with dwindling food, water and morale, Gull Force surrenders at 1530hrs.

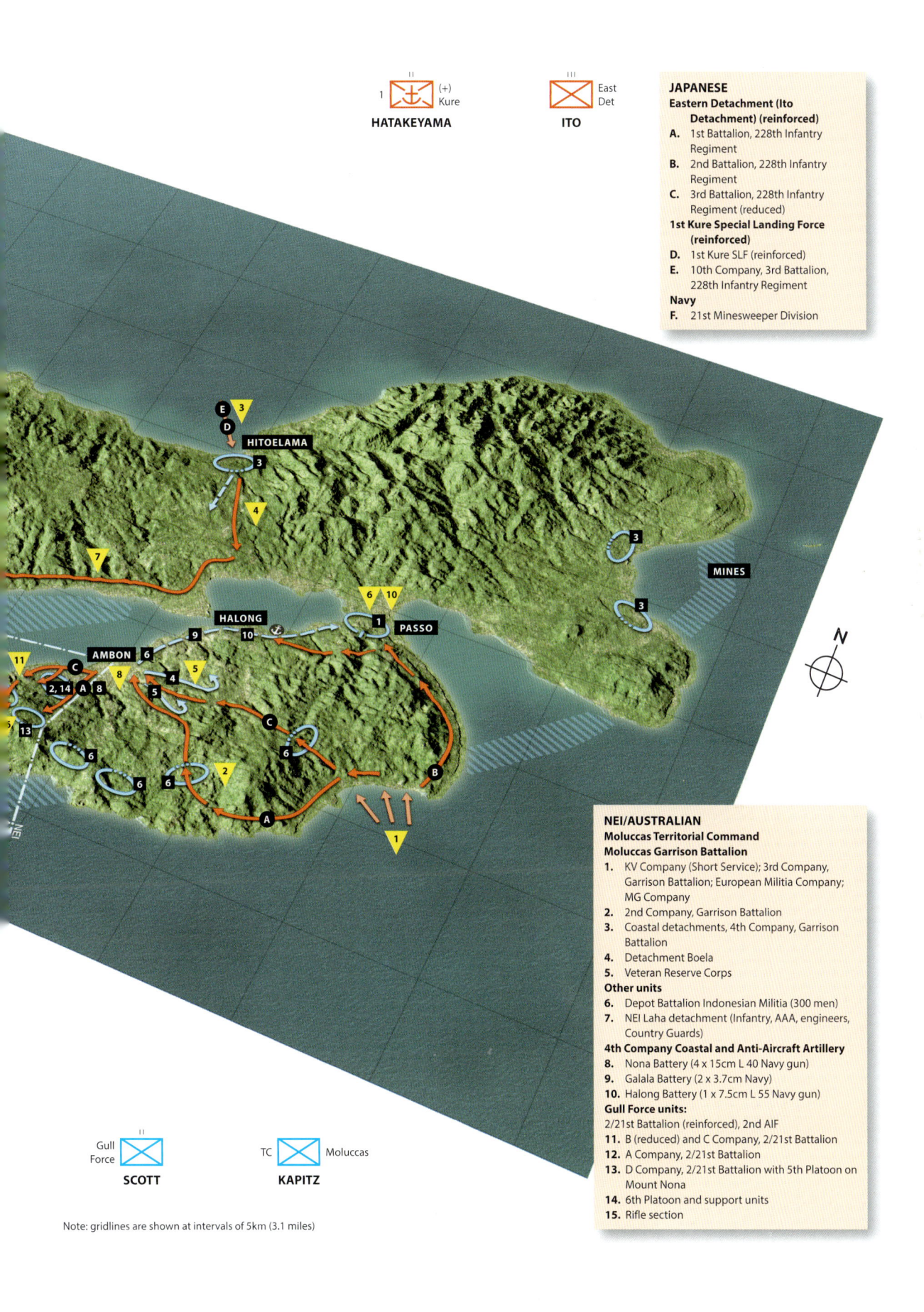

## JAPANESE
**Eastern Detachment (Ito Detachment) (reinforced)**
- **A.** 1st Battalion, 228th Infantry Regiment
- **B.** 2nd Battalion, 228th Infantry Regiment
- **C.** 3rd Battalion, 228th Infantry Regiment (reduced)

**1st Kure Special Landing Force (reinforced)**
- **D.** 1st Kure SLF (reinforced)
- **E.** 10th Company, 3rd Battalion, 228th Infantry Regiment

**Navy**
- **F.** 21st Minesweeper Division

## NEI/AUSTRALIAN
**Moluccas Territorial Command**
**Moluccas Garrison Battalion**
1. KV Company (Short Service); 3rd Company, Garrison Battalion; European Militia Company; MG Company
2. 2nd Company, Garrison Battalion
3. Coastal detachments, 4th Company, Garrison Battalion
4. Detachment Boela
5. Veteran Reserve Corps

**Other units**
6. Depot Battalion Indonesian Militia (300 men)
7. NEI Laha detachment (Infantry, AAA, engineers, Country Guards)

**4th Company Coastal and Anti-Aircraft Artillery**
8. Nona Battery (4 x 15cm L 40 Navy gun)
9. Galala Battery (2 x 3.7cm Navy)
10. Halong Battery (1 x 7.5cm L 55 Navy gun)

**Gull Force units:**
2/21st Battalion (reinforced), 2nd AIF
11. B (reduced) and C Company, 2/21st Battalion
12. A Company, 2/21st Battalion
13. D Company, 2/21st Battalion with 5th Platoon on Mount Nona
14. 6th Platoon and support units
15. Rifle section

HATAKEYAMA — 1 (+) Kure
ITO — East Det
SCOTT — Gull Force
KAPITZ — TC Moluccas

Note: gridlines are shown at intervals of 5km (3.1 miles)

important as a base for air operations against Java. The planned occupation would continue, but the attack from the sea was cancelled. The Sakaguchi Detachment would occupy the city mainly overland, while the IJN would support a small-scale maritime operation along the coast.

After mobilization, the South-Eastern Borneo Garrison Battalion numbered 1,250 men. It was assigned to the defence of two airfields, Kotawaringin and Oelin. On the morning of 10 February 1942, the Japanese overland task force occupied Oelin. The airfield had been destroyed and the NEI defenders had partly withdrawn to Java. Bandjermasin was also occupied that day. The at times highly challenging advance through the jungle took its toll: 80 per cent contracted malaria, and nine men died of this. On 25 February 1942, Oelin was commissioned by the IJN 23rd Air Flotilla as a relay base.

## PALEMBANG (OPERATION *L*)

The main focus of the Japanese offensive against the Netherlands East Indies was, until the first half of February 1942, in the Makassar Strait and the eastern part of the Indonesian archipelago – the clockwise IJN operation. This would change in mid-February with the attack on Palembang, South Sumatra. The Japanese also significantly increased the pace of their offensive. On 14 February 1942, they attacked Palembang, followed on 19 February by the landing on Bali and the next day a landing on Timor. In less than a week, three landing operations and an air raid on Port Darwin severed the last lines of communication between Java and the outside world.

Sumatra is an elongated island (1,750km by 400km) with a central mountain range along the west coast, many volcanoes and on the east coast deep rivers cutting across a wide, swampy coastal plain. The island is covered with old-growth forest. Palembang was the primary city of South Sumatra, with over 109,000 inhabitants in the early 1930s. It lay 105km inland on the Musi River. The main oil wells were at Djambi. The road network was limited. A railway line ran from Palembang, and a partly asphalted, partly gravelled main road featuring several concrete bridges connected it to Bandar Lampung (Oosthaven), some 483km distant. This line of communication was accessible in many places from the east coast via navigable rivers, and was thus vulnerable. The roads around Palembang were mostly causeways through swamps. In Palembang there was no permanent crossing over the Musi River. This crucial connection was maintained by several ferries. The river was navigable by sea-going vessels to Palembang.

Palembang was not only an extremely important springboard for the Japanese advance towards Java, but also an important oil production area. East of the city lay two refineries: Plaju and Sungei Gerong. These refineries jointly processed one-third of total NEI oil production. This was the only source of high-quality jet fuel (100 octane) in the NEI. Palembang I Airfield, also known as Talangbetutu, was 15km north of the city. It was the city's civilian airfield with an L-shaped, paved runway. Palembang II military airfield, still under construction, was *c.* 75km south-west of Palembang. It was brought into use in late December 1941 and early January 1942, and consisted of a large clearing in the jungle. Partly because of this, this airfield remained unknown to the Japanese.

# Operation *L*: the attack on Palembang

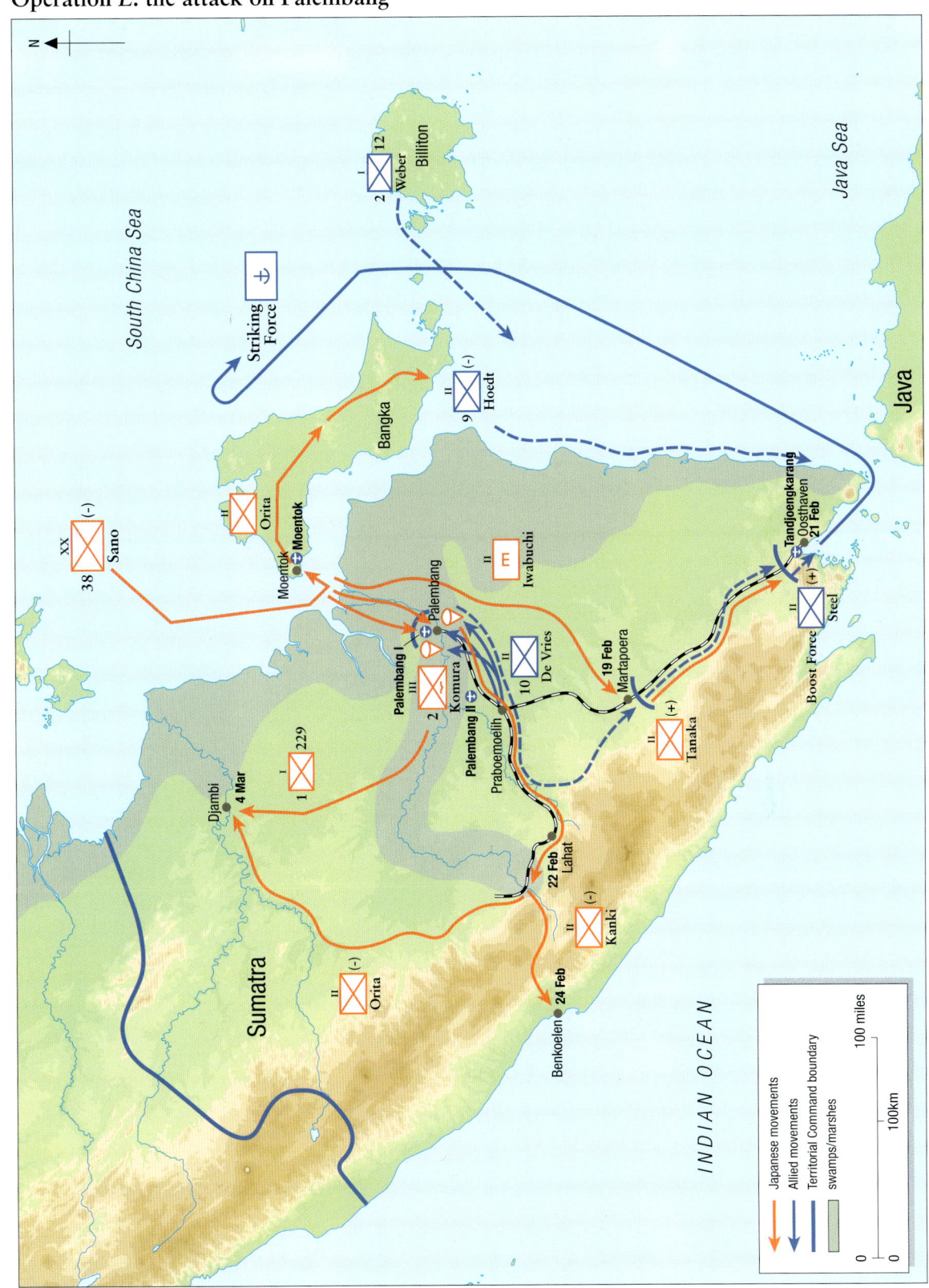

Bandar Lampung (Oosthaven), south Sumatra. On 14 February 1942, the day the Japanese attacked Palembang, the first reinforcements of ground troops from the Middle East destined for Sumatra and Java arrived at Oosthaven. A Mk V1B light tank from the British B Squadron, 3rd King's Own Hussars is seen here on the wharf, while in the background are destroyed trucks, a bus and collapsed buildings. In the late afternoon of 15 February 1942, orders were received to re-embark the 3rd King's Own Hussars. The unit was shipped to Java and saw action as part of Blackforce. (Australian War Memorial)

South Sumatra was defended by Palembang and Djambi Territorial Command. The command consisted of a regional headquarters, the Palembang and Djambi Garrison Battalion of six companies, a Demolition Corps, Palembang Town Guard and Djambi Town Guard. For the defence of the airfield and the oil installations, the territorial troops were reinforced with a machine-gun company and a detachment of artillery of eight 7.5cm guns and two 4cm AA guns. The garrison was also given five APCs: two at Palembang I and three at Palembang II. The total strength was *c.* 1,300 men. The Territorial Commander was Lieutenant-Colonel L.N.W. Vogelesang.

From 16 January 1942, Palembang developed into a major British air base. The bomber squadrons were reorganized into No. 225 (Bomber) Group, stationed at Palembang II. On 1 February 1942, No. 226 (Fighter) Group was formed, based at Palembang I. Ground-based air defence was supplied by: 6th Heavy Anti-Aircraft Artillery Regiment (RA) (reduced), 78th Battery, 35th Light Anti-Aircraft Regiment (RA) and a troop from 89th Light Anti-Aircraft Artillery Battery (RA). Air Commodore Henry J.F. Hunter, commander of No. 225 (Bomber) Group, acted as Air Officer Commanding Palembang.

A small advance party of Australian I Corps had arrived on 26 January 1942 by plane at Jakarta. The GOC, Lieutenant-General J.D. Lavarack, and his chief of staff, Brigadier F.H. Berryman, explored the future deployment area. In South Sumatra, they expected that the Japanese would first occupy Bangka to use as a forward base to gain local maritime and air superiority. Then they would attack the oil refineries using paratroopers. This airborne operation would be combined with an upstream riverine operation. Lavarack therefore advised Wavell to immediately strengthen the defences of the oil refineries and the airfield with an infantry battalion and to hand out rifles to RAF, RAAF and AA gunners. It was decided to send one infantry battalion to the oil refineries and one to the islands of Bangka and Belitung. After the arrival of Australian reinforcements, the defence of Palembang I and Palembang II would be reinforced with a squadron of light tanks.

On 5 February 1942, two RNEI Army field battalions temporarily left Java for Sumatra: the 10th Infantry Battalion went to Palembang, 9th Infantry Battalion (reduced) moved to Bangka island and the reinforced 2nd Company, 12th Infantry Battalion headed to Belitung. Once Australian reinforcements arrived, these battalions would return to Java. The 10th Infantry Battalion's headquarters and three companies were stationed in Praboemoelih. The 1st Company, 10th Infantry Battalion (Javanese) was stationed in Palembang. The choice of Praboemoelih was not ideal. Lying 90km south of Palembang, it was too far from the protected locations to be able to counter-attack quickly. The battalion was provisionally motorized with buses and trucks driven by called-up Indonesian drivers. The 10th Infantry Battalion became available to the Territorial Commander.

Operation *L*, targeting Bangka island and Palembang, had to be postponed twice due to the poor condition of Kuching Airfield and the unavailability of Singkawang II. Kuantan in Malaya should have taken over this role, but this airfield was not made ready in time. Eventually, Operation *L* was scheduled to commence 15 February 1942.

To destroy Allied airpower in Sumatra and also to suppress it on Java, the IJA and IJN divided the operating area across the line Muntok–Palembang on 28 January 1942. The IJA would operate to the west and the IJN to the east of this line. Following preliminary attacks, the 3rd Air Division launched a major offensive over South Sumatra from 6 February to 13 February 1942 to gain local air superiority. The 22nd Air Flotilla flew missions over Bangka and Belitung. The Japanese subsequently believed that the bulk of the Allied aircraft had been destroyed. This turned out to be premature.

Despite the losses suffered, the British still had the following aircraft available on the day of the Japanese landings: 24 Hurricane fighters, 31 Lockheed Hudson light bombers and 36 Bristol Blenheim Mk I and Mk IV light bombers. Many of the Blenheims were unserviceable. Palembang II was not discovered by the Japanese as a base, and was therefore available for the deployment of fighter aircraft and bombers. All in all, there was no question of Japanese air supremacy.

Operation *L*, as predicted by Lieutenant-General Lavarack, was a combined airborne and amphibious/riverine attack. The IJA had specifically trained the 1st Raiding Group (an airborne unit) for the conquest of Palembang. The 1st Raiding Regiment turned out to be unavailable because it had lost armament and equipment in a shipping accident in early January 1942 and had also been struck by an outbreak of paratyphoid fever. As a result, the 2nd Raiding Regiment, still in training, was deployed. A raiding regiment consisted of four companies of 160 men and thus actually had the strength of a battalion.

The 1st Raiding Group was not strong enough to simultaneously attack and hold the three chosen objectives, the airfield and the two refineries. Southern Army prioritized the capture of the airfield. If possible, the refineries were to be captured before the Allies could destroy them. But even now, the available forces were too small for three objectives. Moreover, the group had to hold the objectives until the arrival off the main force of the 38th Division (scheduled for L+2, Day L marking the amphibious landing on Bangka). The airborne landing was scheduled for L-1.

The 38th Division was tasked with capturing Palembang city. The losses it suffered during the taking of Hong Kong had since been made good. Nevertheless, the division was not at full strength. Two detachments were formed from its ranks, to be deployed elsewhere: the Eastern Detachment and Shoji Detachment. For the Palembang operation, the 38th Division therefore consisted of a core of four infantry battalions of the 229th Infantry Regiment. An independent transport battalion, a shipping engineer regiment and other specialist units, including an oil-drilling unit, were placed under its control.

Under Vice Admiral Jisaburo Ozawa, the IJN provided large-scale maritime support to Operation *L*. Ozawa's Malaya Unit (First Southern

A Japanese postcard published by the Army Art Association based on a war painting by Goro Tsuruta, 'The Warrior God descended in Palembang'. The IJA and IJN engaged renowned Japanese artists to lay down the Sino-Japanese War and the Pacific War in monumental realistic paintings in Western style (*yoga*) as opposed to Japanese style (*nihonga*). These paintings of the war campaigns were shown to the Japanese public in large-scale exhibitions. (NARA, public domain)

Japanese paratroopers jumping from Army Type 100 Transport Model 1 (Mitsubishi Ki-57) planes, Allied codename Topsy. This aircraft had a crew of four and could carry 11 paratroopers. This is probably the 3rd Company, 2nd Raiding Regiment (totalling 90 men) that jumped on 15 February 1942 onto Palembang I Airfield. (Keystone-France\Gamma-Rapho via Getty Images)

Expeditionary Fleet) provided the Main Unit and two Escort units. The 1st Air Unit and the 22nd Air Flotilla provided air support to the transport fleet. The 2nd Air Unit provided air support to the transport fleet, guarded the Bangka and Palembang anchorage, and supported the operation upstream of the rivers. The 4th Carrier Division formed the 3rd Air Unit and had to guard against Allied ships. The 9th Base Force delivered the river-ascending unit.

On Saturday morning, 14 February 1942 at 1126hrs, the paratroopers of the 2nd Raiding Regiment jumped out of 25 transport aircraft of the Raiding Air Unit. At Palembang I the first echelon, consisting of the regimental headquarters, signal unit, 4th Company and half the 2nd Company (180 men), landed *c.* 3km to the south-east, and two platoons of 2nd company (60 men) landed immediately west of Palembang I. The airfield defenders were kept in check by an aerial bombardment and strafing, which would give the paratroopers enough time to arm and regroup after landing. The airborne operation was not flawless. British fighter planes attacked twice, but were driven off on both occasions. The paratroopers did not jump with their weapons and ammunition; these were dropped separately in containers. Due to the difficult terrain, the paratroopers often failed to recover these containers. Often armed only with pistols and grenades, they could not develop enough firepower to overcome the resistance quickly and take the airfield. Some paratroopers armed with an LMG erected a roadblock 8km from the city on the way to the airfield, thereby hindering communications between Palembang and the airfield.

The Palembang I garrison consisted of a battery from 15th Heavy Anti-Aircraft Regiment with eight 3.7in. guns, a section from 78th Battery and a troop from 89th Battery (both from 35th Light Anti-Aircraft Regiment) with eight 40mm Bofors, 150 RNEI Army men with two APCs and the defence sections (ground defence detachments) of Nos. 258 and 605 (Fighter) squadrons (about 60 men). Wing Commander H.G. Maguire acted as base commander on Saturday due to the senior officer being ill. The British AA gunners were able to take on the security of their own positions by forming ground defence squads and anti-paratroop patrols. The personnel had received weapons and ground defence training and had familiarized themselves with the wider environment of their gun positions. The airfield defenders fiercely opposed the attacking paratroopers all day. Once the AA artillery had almost used up its limited ammunition stocks against air and ground targets, it was partially evacuated to Palembang under cover of the ground defence squads. With about 70 men left, Wing Commander Maguire saw no way of defending the airfield against night attacks. He and his men withdrew north-west in trucks shortly before nightfall. The runways, although mined, were not destroyed, as the store containing the detonators had burnt down during the attack. The airfield fell into Japanese hands undamaged.

The refineries were attacked by the 1st Company, 2nd Raiding Regiment at 1130hrs. Sixty men landed at Plaju, and the 3rd Platoon (39 men) jumped south-east of Sungei Gerong. Palembang II, unknown to the Japanese, was therefore not attacked. Around noon, air support for the airborne troops ceased.

The refineries were arranged for all-round defence with a garrison of approximately 150 men at each of them. The focus was on repelling an attack from the Musi River. However, the Japanese attack came from the south. At Plaju Refinery, the majority of the paratroopers landed to the south-west, while some landed in the refinery. They established themselves at the site. The NEI defenders received reinforcements from a British anti-paratroop squad (20 men) of AA gunners, and started a sweep. The Town Guard platoon cleared the residential area west of the refinery. At the beginning of the afternoon, the reinforced Menadonese 2nd Company, 10th Infantry Battalion (reduced) arrived from Praboemoelih. By evening, this company had almost cleared the complex, and the next day prepared to mop up the last remaining group of about 15 men. The Japanese platoon attack on Sungei Gerong Refinery was immediately repelled. On 14 February 1942, the Japanese reported losses of 39 paratroopers killed in action and 48 wounded out of the 329 men who jumped.

Lieutenant-Colonel Vogelesang directed one platoon (reduced) of territorial troops in two armoured cars and the reinforced 1st Company, 10th Infantry Battalion towards Palembang I. The Town Guard was ordered to take up a blocking position north of the city. The counter-attack by 1st Company, 10th Infantry Battalion only started at around 1630hrs. The core of 10th Infantry Battalion at Praboemoelih and part of Plaju's garrison was on exercise that morning. As a result, the response started late. On the advice of Brigadier C.S. Steele, Chief Engineer of Australian I Corps, who was touring South Sumatra, the RAF organized a bridgehead with armed RAF personnel at the Musi ferry. Several uncoordinated actions to reach Palembang I failed at the Japanese roadblock. The counter-attack executed by 1st Company, 10th Infantry Battalion did not go smoothly, but in the afternoon it cleared the roadblock. Its advance was, however, halted due to nightfall, with the intent of resuming it the next morning. During the day, the NEI territorial commander felt optimistic about the course of the battle. The Japanese attack on the refineries had failed. Although Palembang I had fallen into Japanese hands after lengthy resistance, the planned counter-attack stood a good chance of success.

Confusion reigned at RAF HQ Palembang that morning. Air Commodore Hunter gave the order to evacuate Palembang I and move the fighters back to Palembang II. He was then ordered to move the fighter aircraft to Jakarta. This order was revoked by ABDA-AIR around noon, and the aircraft returned. The RAF HQ in Palembang was cleared, and in the early afternoon reoccupied. However, its transmitter and the codes had been destroyed.

ABDACOM also responded at sea. The Japanese convoy destined for South Sumatra left Cam Ranh Bay on 9 and 10 February 1942 and was reconnoitred on the morning of 13 February. It was then attacked by British aircraft from Palembang in the evening of the same day and the following morning. The Japanese suffered no losses. The Allied naval squadron, the

Five Menadonese riflemen of the 2nd Company, 10th Infantry Battalion at Palembang. This company counter-attacked and expelled the Japanese paratroopers from Plaju Refinery. In the background, the burning oil refinery can be seen. The soldiers are armed with the M95 repeating carbine, *klewang* swords and grenades. They wear the grey-green field dress Model 1937 with puttees, and the steel helmet with leather neck flap (for protection against the sun). (Museum Bronbeek)

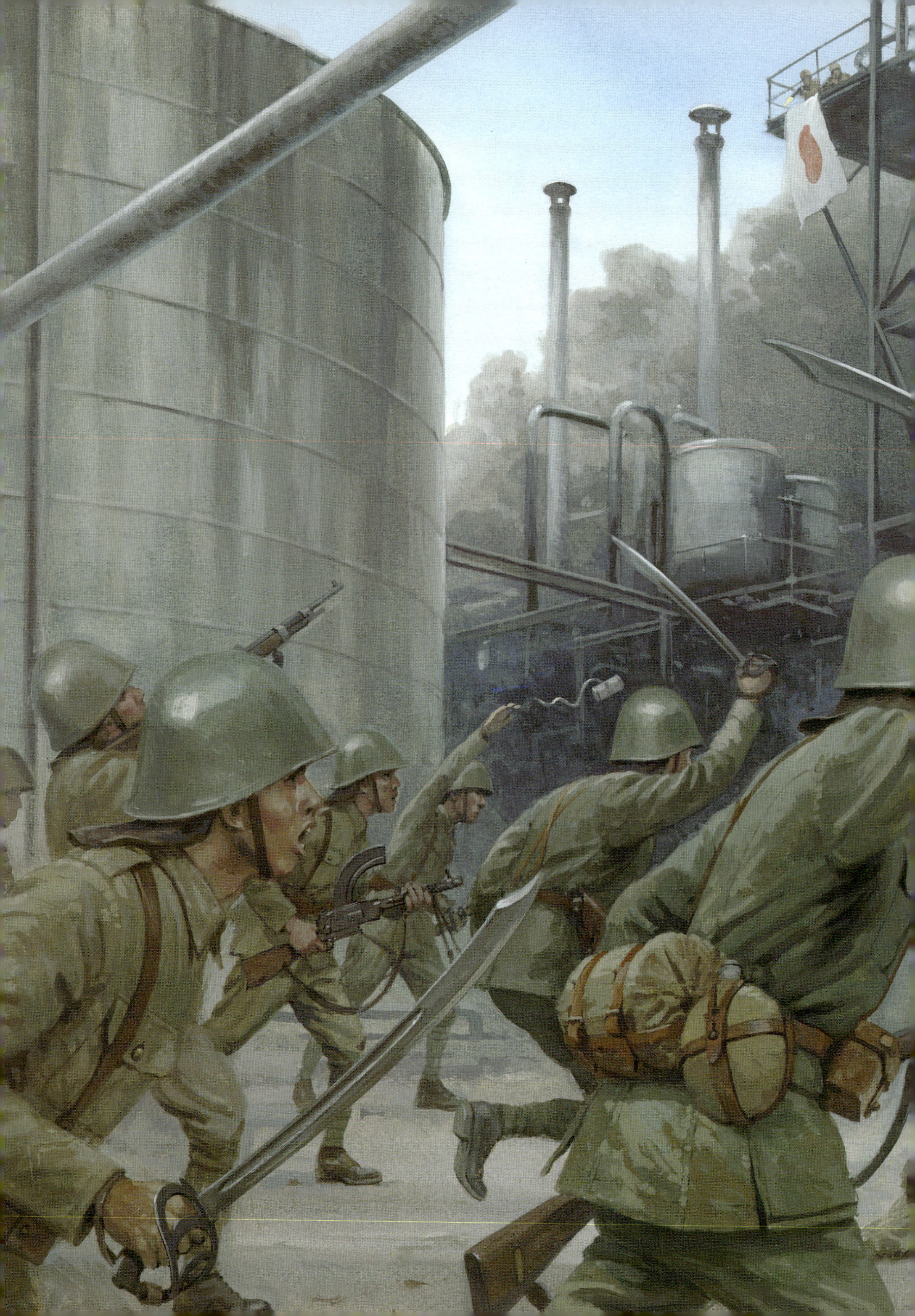

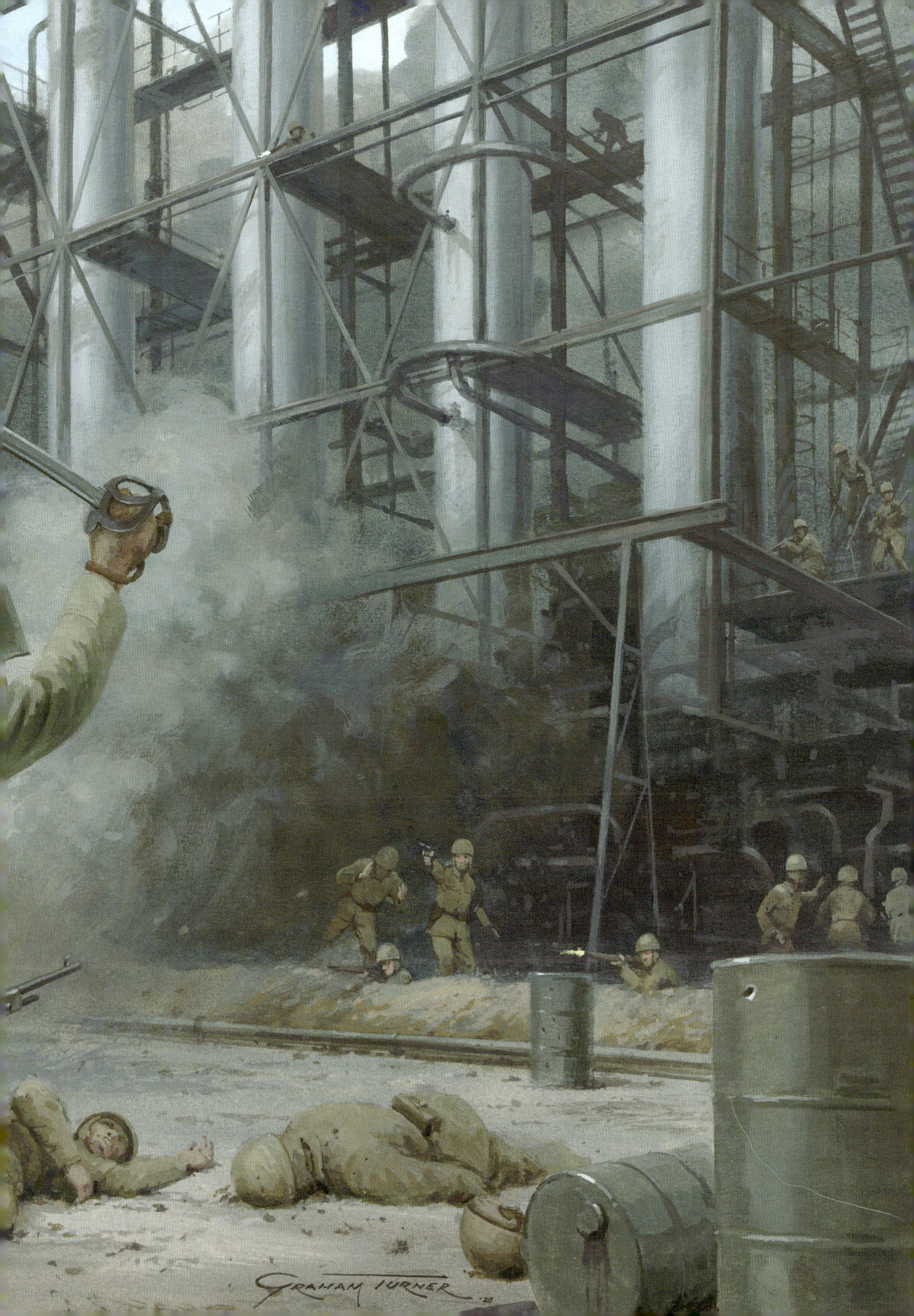
GRAHAM TURNER
'20

**NEI COUNTER-ATTACK AT PLAJU REFINERY, PALEMBANG, 14 FEBRUARY 1942 (PP. 60–61)**

For the IJA airborne attack on the two refineries of Plaju and Sungei Gerong at Palembang on 14 February 1942, the battalion-sized airborne 2nd Raiding Regiment could only allocate the 1st Company (less elements, 99 men).

The IJA paratroopers, led by company commander 1st Lieutenant Nakao, jumped at the refineries at 0930hrs local (South Sumatra) time. Sixty men landed at Plaju Refinery, the majority to its south-west while some did land in the refinery itself. They manage to establish themselves on the site and set up a defence in shelter trenches, behind the earth banks around the oil tanks, on top of the oil tanks and in the refinery upper platforms.

At around 1230hrs, the reinforced Menadonese 2nd Company, 10th Infantry Battalion under Captain J.H.M.U.L.E. Ohl arrived. He also had at his disposal from 4th Company, 10th Infantry Battalion; two MMG platoons (eight Vickers 6.5mm MGs); one mortar section (two 81mm mortars); and an AT rifle group (two 20mm AT rifles). Along the Moesi River, Ohl formed a fire base of one MMG platoon and one AT rifle to cover his rear and left flank. His right flank was covered by a platoon of Town Guards. Upon the arrival of a platoon from the Javanese 3rd Company, 10th Infantry Battalion, Ohl reorganized his attack force into three reinforced platoons. His total strength was now 312 men (excluding the Town Guards).

Capt Ohl began his sweep at 1320hrs. Initially, the advance was slow due to Japanese sniper fire. With the arrival of reinforcements, his attack gained momentum, and the Japanese were expelled from an oil tank park.

This scene shows the NEI assault at the end of the afternoon on the Plaju distillation unit by the right forward platoon under 2nd Lieutenant E.J. van Blommestein with *klewangs* drawn. The assault was covered by mortar fire, and MMG fire aimed at the Japanese positions in the towers and among the oil tanks. Further cover was provided by smoke from a burning solar tank. On Van Blommestein's left was the reserve platoon commanded by Captain Ohl.

The assaulting Menadonese soldiers (**1**) are armed with M.95 carbines (**2**) and *klewangs* (**3**). In the background, a soldier throws a hand grenade (**4**). When thrown, the grenade's 2m-long safety band unravelled, causing the safety pin to be pulled out in flight. The grenade would explode on impact. In the centre of our scene, a gunner carries the standard RNEI Army LMG (**5**), the magazine-fed 6.5 x 53.5mm M.15 Madsen (*karabijnmitrailleur*). The Japanese paratroopers are beginning to retreat (**6**).

After the recapture of the refinery, Lieutenant Van Blommestein, Menadonese Private 1st Class Pelealuw and Menadonese Private Buntua each climbed a tower of the refinery and lowered the three Japanese flags (**7**) under intense Japanese fire.

That evening, at 2100hrs, an NEI attempt to extinguish the last Japanese resistance of about 15 men using hand grenades failed. The attack left the 10th Infantry Battalion with at least one NCO killed and one man seriously injured.

A number of oil tanks caught fire at the refinery on account of the mortar fire. The fire quickly spread due to the strong wind. By midnight, the tank site was ablaze. The troops prepared to mop up the paratroopers in the swamp forest in the early morning, but at 0330hrs Captain Ohl received orders to withdraw. The refinery and its extensive supplies fell into Japanese hands, with only minor damage to the installations.

Combined Striking Force, was also deployed against the Japanese fleet. Vice Admiral Ozawa deployed his air units against this threat. Without air cover and with the element of surprise lost, Doorman decided to cancel the action.

After midnight on 15 February 1942, the amphibious/riverine part of Operation *L* commenced with the arrival of the Japanese transport ships at the anchorage at Muntok, Bangka. The Muntok landing unit of 1st Battalion (reduced), 229th Infantry Regiment landed at Muntok at 0225hrs and quickly took the city and Muntok Airfield. The latter was immediately expanded by the 33rd Airfield Company. The NEI units on Bangka and Belitung were ordered to withdraw to Java. The river-ascending units left for the Musi Delta and reached the mouth of the river by morning. The Iwabuchi Unit on the left wing advanced by the Saleh River past Palembang towards Martapura. The IJN supported this advance with minesweeping operations in the rivers. The river-ascending units were repeatedly attacked by RAF planes from Palembang II. The Japanese suffered only minor losses. Japanese air coverage was limited that day due to commitments elsewhere. The IJN was in action against the Combined Striking Force, while the Third Air Force supported the second airborne landing. The Military Aviation Service and FEAF flew bomber missions against the Japanese landing fleet near Muntok, but enjoyed little success.

The repeated air strikes could not halt the Japanese river-ascending units. This eventually made Palembang untenable. During the night of 15 February, Palembang received reports from coastguards about the Japanese fleet approaching the Musi, the disembarkation in landing craft and the advance up the Musi. The NEI territorial commander then ordered the destruction of the oil refineries and the withdrawal of troops to Palembang at approximately 0300hrs. The artillery battery located at Pradjen on the Musi had to be destroyed and evacuated. Lieutenant-Colonel Vogelesang himself moved his command post to the east bank. Sungei Gerong Refinery was thoroughly destroyed, but Plaju, on the other hand, fell into Japanese hands with large stocks of oil and aviation fuel and only minor damage to its installations. A thorough destruction of Plaju had been prepared but not carried out, as the destruction troops were not on site on 15 February 1942: the territorial commander had forbidden its destruction on 14 February and recalled the unit to Palembang. At 1100hrs, the territorial commander prematurely ordered the telephone exchange to be destroyed, and retreated to Lahat. The Territorial Command fell apart.

The withdrawal order applied to troops south-east of the Musi, not to the north of Palembang. The order to recapture Palembang I Airfield using 1st Company, 10th Infantry Battalion was confirmed by the territorial commander on the morning of 15 February 1942. Shortly after noon, the Japanese third echelon, comprising 3rd Company, 2nd Raiding Regiment (90 men), jumped over Palembang I. The 10th Infantry Battalion's commander, Major B.P. de Vries, was also informed that the Japanese landing troops had approached up to 8km via the Palembang River. He then decided to call off the counter-attack and withdrew his troops to the east bank of the Musi.

An IJA Type 99 Kawasaki Ki-48 twin-engined light bomber. During the fighting around Palembang, some Japanese troops were taken prisoner. On 13 February 1942, in a last major preparatory air raid on Palembang, the Japanese 3rd Air Division lost three aircraft to British planes: two IJA Type 1 fighters and one IJA Type 99 Kawasaki Ki-48 from Ipoh Airfield (Malaya). Of the latter, three of the four crew members were captured, all wounded. The first pilot was killed. The second pilot, probably the navigator, was interrogated by the Dutch. The next day, the same interpreter questioned a (hospitalized) Japanese paratrooper prisoner. Captured Japanese documents and interrogation reports were sent to Java. The fate of the Japanese prisoners of war is unknown. (Public domain)

**ABOVE LEFT**
Japanese paratroopers of the 1st Company, 2nd Raiding Regiment placed flags on three of the four distillation towers of Reformplant II at the Plaju Refinery near Palembang. In the NEI counter-attack, these flags were removed by an officer and two Menadonese soldiers of 2nd Company, 10th Infantry Battalion. Here, Indonesian and European soldiers of this unit proudly display one of these flags, having returned to Jakarta (Java) from Sumatra, February 1942. (Beeldbank WW2 – NIOD)

**ABOVE RIGHT**
The riverine component of the assault on Palembang comprised an advance by three units up three rivers, two of which were ordered to make contact with the paratroopers. The burning oil refineries along the Musi River can be seen here. This unit is most likely the one that ascended the Musi River (the central column), or the follow-on 38th Division troops. (ullstein bild via Getty Images)

The RAF retreated to Palembang II. Air Commodore Hunter soon also had Palembang II cleared. The RAF then withdrew to Bandar Lampung by road and rail. This retreat was chaotic. Equipment and unit cohesion were both partly lost. In contrast, the 6th Heavy Anti-Aircraft Regiment and 10th Infantry Battalion, with 400–500 territorial troops, withdrew in an orderly manner, although 6th Heavy Anti-Aircraft Regiment subsequently had to leave behind the remaining guns. The 10th Infantry Battalion conducted a rearguard action against the Iwabuchi Unit on 18 February 1942 in Martapura. The Japanese failed to cut off the retreat route in time. After a short firefight, 10th Infantry Battalion broke off the action.

Contrary to reports, Japanese river-ascending units did not reach Palembang until the early evening of 15 February 1942. That evening, overland contact with the 2nd Raiding Regiment at Palembang I was established. On the 16th, contact was made with the paratroopers at the oil refineries. In the early evening of 16 February, the Main Unit of 38th Division anchored at the mouth of the Musi River, but did not reach Palembang before the 20th. Palembang II was only discovered by the Japanese on 16 February.

While the Battle of Palembang was progressing, the first Commonwealth reinforcements arrived in Bandar Lampung. On 14 February 1942, Convoy JS 1, bearing the British 7th Armoured Brigade, arrived. The next day, Convoy JS 2 anchored in Bandar Lampung. It consisted of one ship, the HMT *Orcades*, with the advance guard of the Australian 7th Division. Although these units were missing some of their heavy equipment, a large proportion of the troops were immediately disembarked. Australian Brigadier C.S. Steele had arrived from Palembang in Bandar Lampung on the morning of 15 February 1942. Using the available forces, he formed an ad hoc unit for the defence of Bandar Lampung: Boost Force. It consisted of B Squadron, 3rd King's Own Hussars; 95th Battery, 48th Light Anti-Aircraft Regiment (RA); and five improvised RAF rifle companies each approximately 100 men strong.

In the late afternoon of 15 February 1942, Allied forces in Singapore surrendered. The fall of Singapore, as ABDACOM wired, led to a 'change in programme'. The troops that had arrived at Bandar Lampung were ordered not to disembark. Convoys JS 1 and JS 2 had to sail to Tanjung Priok and await further orders there. ABDA-AIR ordered the evacuation of RAF personnel via Bandar Lampung. The troops reboarded their ships. South Sumatra was thus given up relatively quickly by ABDACOM.

During the fighting at Palembang and also in the retreat, the NEI troops, in particular the territorial ones, showed a certain 'reluctance to be deployed'. In the counter-attack at Plaju, a platoon of 3rd Company, 10th Infantry Battalion refused to advance. The latter was attributed to the failures of the platoon commander.

South Sumatra was lost in two days. The pincer from the west had closed around Java. Within a few days, the pincer from the east would encircle it, too. The main island of the Netherlands East Indies was surrounded and no longer tenable.

## BALI

At 0100hrs on 19 February 1942, the 3rd Battalion (reduced), 1st Formosan Infantry Regiment, a mountain artillery section and an independent engineers platoon of the 48th Division landed on the south coast of Bali. The 1st Base Unit of the IJN provided the escort. Documents were found on Tarakan indicating that Bali's airfield was in good condition. In addition, the location was extremely favourable. From Bali it was not only possible to conduct the air campaign against East Java, but also to cut off the supply route from Australia. The IJN 23rd Air Flotilla then made a strong case to include Bali again in the operation plan. It was agreed to do so at the conference in Manila on 28 January 1942.

Bali was defended by the Prajoda Corps, an Indonesian auxiliary battalion-sized unit with some European officers and NCOs. After the Japanese landing, this corps disintegrated due to widespread desertion. Den Pasar Airfield fell quickly, almost intact, into Japanese hands. It was already in use the next day. The 23rd Air Flotilla headquarters was moved from Balikpapan to Bali on 26 February 1942.

ABDACOM reacted with violent air raids on the two Japanese transport ships during the disembarkation of troops and supplies. Both ships were damaged, one heavily. The Combined Striking Force was also deployed against this serious threat on the eastern flank. It attacked the Japanese landing fleet with an unsuccessful hit-and-run attack on the night of 19/20 February 1942. Above all, the action came too late. The Japanese troops had already reached their ground objectives.

HMT *Orcades* arrived from the Middle East with 3,391 troops of the Australian 7th Division in Tanjung Priok on 16 February 1942. Only part of the division disembarked on 18 February; General Wavell planned to use them for airfield defence. The troops shown here on the gangplank of HMT *Orcades* may be from 2/2nd Pioneer Battalion; the two soldiers in the foreground are carrying a cased Bren LMG. They formed Blackforce with other Australian units and troops. The *Orcades* departed on 21 March 1942 as Convoy SJ 6 (Batavia–Colombo) with 3,500 personnel. On 10 October 1942, the *Orcades* was sunk by a German submarine. (Australian War Memorial)

## TIMOR

The island of Timor was politically divided into Dutch and Portuguese parts. The eastern part was Portuguese and its capital was Dilly. The western part was Dutch, with a small Portuguese enclave on the north-west coast, and its capital was Kupang. The island has a length of 476km and is 102km wide. It is very mountainous and covered with tropical dry forests. The road network was limited. In the Dutch part, one unpaved main connecting road (about 4–5m wide) ran from Kupang to the Portuguese border. The roadside terrain was unsuitable for motor vehicles due to coral and swamps. Penfoei Airfield was located about 4km north-east of Kupang.

The NEI semi-motorized MG and Infantry Gun companies were reorganized in 1940 into fully mechanized and motorized AT and AA companies (*afdeling Pantser- en Luchtafweer*). The latter provided anti-tank and mobile anti-aircraft defence for the regiments. The AA platoon (57 men) was equipped with nine M30 Colt 12.7mm (.50-cal.) heavy AA MGs each on a pivot gun carriage on the back of a light open Chevrolet truck. The gun crew was not protected against incoming fire. In this photo, a section of three trucks with AA MGs and an ammunition truck can be seen. By late 1938, the RNEI Army regarded the 12.7mm AA MG as obsolete. They were to be replaced by 2cm guns, but during the Japanese offensive the old AA MGs were still widely used. (Netherlands Institute of Military History)

The Timor and Dependencies Territorial Command consisted of a regional headquarters and the Timor and Dependencies Garrison Battalion of 27 brigades (19 men per brigade), of which 21 brigades were stationed on Timor. The territorial commander was Lieutenant-Colonel W.E.C. Detiger. In addition, the garrison had the standard three APCs. Its mission was to maintain neutrality and prevent a Japanese landing. Its total strength was *c.* 500 men. The territorial troops were still organized as internal security troops and lacked striking power and firepower against a modern organized armed force.

Australia stationed a flight (four Hudsons) of No. 2 Squadron RAAF and Sparrow Force on Timor. Sparrow Force consisted of 2/40th Battalion, 2/1st Heavy Battery (RAA) and some support and service units under Lieutenant-Colonel W.W. Leggatt. He also had four RAAF armoured vehicles at his disposal. The strength was about 1,250 men. In the American-Dutch-British discussions in 1941, it was agreed that land forces would be commanded by the countries in which they would operate. Timor was an exception to this. The island would come under Australian command at the outbreak of hostilities.

The Dutch believed that a large-scale landing was only possible in Kupang Bay. Lieutenant-Colonel Leggatt questioned this. Nevertheless, he based his defence on a direct coastal defence with the NEI troops and A and B companies, 2/40th Battalion west and east of Kupang respectively and a static coastal battery of two 6in. naval guns. C Company, 2/40th Battalion was located at Penfoei Airfield, and the motorized D Company served as a mobile defence at Babaoe, on the connecting road 10km east of Kupang.

Penfoei was attacked from the air from 26 January 1942. As a result, the airfield was no longer operational by the end of January. It was subsequently used as a stopover point. The rationale for the presence of Australian ground forces had thus been invalidated. However, ABDACOM decided not to evacuate Timor, but to strengthen it with air and ground forces. Of these, only an Australian brigade HQ with Brigadier W.C.D. Veale and the British 79th Battery (reduced), 21st Light Anti-Aircraft Regiment (RA) arrived. The rest of the reinforcements were attacked by Japanese planes at sea en route and returned to Port Darwin.

The Japanese operational plan for Timor consisted of an amphibious landing on the south coast at Kupang and near Dilly (East Timor) by the Ito (Eastern) Detachment. This detachment would sail out from Ambon in five transport ships. Protection was provided by the Eastern Attack Unit consisting of the 5th Cruiser Division as Support Unit, and the 2nd Escort Unit consisting of the 2nd Destroyer Squadron. The 1001 Unit, or 3rd Yokosuka SLF (an IJN paratrooper unit), would carry out an airborne assault at Penfoei. The 3rd Yokosuka SLF was originally intended for the operation against Balikpapan, but its jump was cancelled.

Admiral Isoroku Yamamoto, Commander-in-Chief Combined Fleet, placed the core of the IJN, the Carrier Task Force, less the 5th Carrier Division, at the disposal of the Southern Task Force as part of the Phase III operations on 8 February 1942. The Southern Task Force deployed the aircraft carriers for an air strike on Port Darwin (Mobile Operation I) and for operations south of Java (Mobile Operation II). On Thursday morning, 19 February 1942, 188 planes from the four Carrier Task Force aircraft carriers supported by 54 planes from the 21st Air Flotilla of Kendari and Ambon attacked the north Australian port city of Darwin. The latter was an important but poorly equipped base for operations in the Netherlands East Indies. With the devastating air strike, it was put out of action for the time being.

In the early hours (0235 and 0315) of Friday, 20 February 1942, troops from the Eastern Detachment landed in three areas on the undefended south coast of Timor. Eastern Detachment consisted of the 1st and 3rd battalions, 228th Infantry Regiment; the 2nd Battalion, 38th Mountain Artillery Regiment; and a light tank company. The IJN delivered two platoons of the 1st Sasebo SLF and the 118 remaining troops of the 3rd Yokosuka SLF. In three columns operating side by side, the detachment used trails, tracks and an improved motor road to cross the mountain range northwards towards Kupang and Penfoei. It was like a repeat of the attack on Ambon. On 22 February 1942, a fourth landing took place at Tenau, which included tanks, among other things.

After the amphibious landing, Leggatt decided to vacate and destroy the airfield. D Company took up a blocking position south of Kupang on the road to Baoen to slow the Japanese advance. Along the main connecting road, his line of communication, Leggatt wanted to instigate a delaying action. In the open terrain behind Tjamplong (45km east of Kupang), he intended to make a final stand. This was where his firepower, in the form of .303-cal. machine guns and 3in. mortars, would come into its own.

The NEI Kupang Detachment cleared their positions on the coast and assembled south of Kupang. Part of it had to take up a blocking position on the Baoen–Kupang road and liaise with D Company. No further orders from the territorial commander were forthcoming. At the end of the afternoon, Captain A.L. van Mastrigt took command of the Kupang Detachment (189 men) and moved towards Penfoei. In the morning of 21 February 1942, he and his second-in-command were, however, wounded by friendly Australian fire, and dropped out of the line. Their successor, a youthful, nervous ensign, did not join the Australians but dissolved the detachment. The RNEI Army's role had been played out before it had even started.

At 1045hrs, the airborne landing by 450 Japanese paratroopers from the HQ, 1st and 3rd companies, 3rd Yokosuka SLF took place on a meadow about 12km from their objective: the airfield. This drop zone was chosen because of the heavy losses at Menado, where the paratroopers jumped directly above the objective. The paratroopers blocked the main road at Babaoe. This unexpectedly threatened Sparrow Force in its rear, and cut off its intended retreat route. Leggatt responded by concentrating his troops west of Babaoe and trying to force his way through. Meanwhile, he failed to establish radio communications with Australian troops under Brigadier Veale in Tjamplong. As a result, there was no coordinated joint action against the Japanese blockade. However, because of their encounter with the Australian troops, the paratroopers were unable to reach the airfield.

This Japanese SLF petty officer is dressed in the special two-piece uniform with extra pockets worn by IJN paratroopers. Instead of jump boots, however, he wears field shoes with puttees. On the upper right sleeve can be seen his trade badge/rank insignia in red on dark blue. This model of trade badge was officially worn until November 1942. The paratrooper also wears a leather belt and two canvas ammunition bandoleers. Around his neck he wears a bag containing the ashes of a killed comrade. He is armed with a 6.5mm Model 38 (1905) Arisaka repeating carbine with Model 30 (1897) bayonet mounted. (Public domain)

The next day, at 1024hrs, the second echelon of some 250 men from 2nd Company, 3rd Yokosuka SLF jumped onto the same drop zone. Leggatt counter-attacked and succeeded in recapturing Babaoe. However, the Eastern Detachment's right attack unit, the reinforced 2nd Company, 1st Battalion (206 men), reached the main road at the end of the day and formed a new roadblock east of Babaoe. Once again, the Australian retreat route had been cut.

In the afternoon of 22 February 1942, Sparrow Force managed to finally open the road, having attacked several times during the morning. The Japanese vanguard from Kupang had, however, caught up, followed the next morning by the reinforced 1st Battalion, 228th Infantry Regiment with light tanks. Lieutenant-Colonel Leggatt was forced to surrender.

Sparrow Force's combat strength suffered from declining morale and an increasing disease rate (30 per cent). Morale declined under Japanese air strikes, Japanese successes elsewhere, the lack of air support and the knowledge that reinforcements would not be forthcoming. Tactically speaking, communication was 'very difficult to maintain in this type of country'. Leggatt recognized this control issue. Partly for this reason, he wanted to fight it out in the open area near Tjamplong. He also deployed his troops on 21 and 22 February 1942 in a fragmented manner, thus losing valuable time – time that Leggatt did not have in view of the Japanese advance in his rear from Kupang. He could have kept a large reserve against this anticipated threat. The troops showed a lack of willingness to fight on 20 and 21 February 1942: at this stage, they 'were not very confident and were apt to withdraw when single shots were fired in their vicinity'. This could be attributed to a lack of combat experience. On 22 February 1942, nervousness resulted in panic. Despite these shortcomings, Sparrow Force had stood firm. Its casualties amounted to 150 men killed or wounded, while 200 were missing. The 3rd Yokosuka SLF suffered 38 killed and 40 to 50 wounded. The Eastern Detachment reported 67 killed and 56 wounded. The Japanese imprisoned 1,136 men: 179 British, 934 Australians and 23 Dutch.

At the same time as the attack on Kupang, the Eastern Detachment also attacked Dilly, the capital of Portuguese Timor. Dilly had been occupied on 17 December 1941 by a combined NEI-Australian detachment under Dutch leadership. The RNEI Army had urged this step to prevent Japan from establishing an air base there, from which it would be able to reach the airfields at Makassar and Kendari, directly threaten Ambon and Darwin, and control the lines of communication between the Netherlands East Indies and Australia.

The NEI-Australian expedition consisted of the so-called NEI Detachment Q of the reinforced Menadonese 3rd Company, 8th Infantry Battalion from Java, a battery of four 7.5cm L30 field guns, a detachment of engineers and some service personnel. It was reinforced by six brigades from the Kupang Garrison Battalion. The Australians detached the 2nd Independent Company, a commando unit (270 men). The Dutch contingent totalled 604 men. The expedition's commander was Lieutenant-Colonel N.L.W. van Straten. The NEI detachment defended the port of Dilly and the airfield in positions without depth. As a commando unit, the 2nd Independent Company was not suited to static defence. It was designated as the reserve and located in the mountains 4km south-west of Dilly. One section was stationed at the airfield.

The presence of NEI and Australian troops in Portuguese Timor made Japan question how it would deal with this neutral territory. The Imperial General HQ wanted to avoid conflict with Portugal. However, the Southern Army (IJA) and Southern Task Force (IJN) agreed that Allied forces in Dilly posed a threat to the attack on Kupang. They had to be driven out. Dilly thereafter had to remain in Japanese hands as an important base for operations against Darwin. The Sixteenth Army objected to the simultaneous actions on Timor. It wanted to concentrate its forces on the conquest of Kupang. It referred to the unsuccessful attack on Laha in the operation against Ambon. The Imperial General HQ ended this discussion.

On 20 February 1942, the Eastern Detachment with the reinforced 2nd Battalion, 228th Infantry Regiment (led by regimental commander Colonel Sadashichi Doi) planned a direct surprise attack on Dilly. This failed due to NEI artillery and machine-gun fire. Colonel Doi modified his plan and landed just under a kilometre to the west. The amphibious landing took place at 0218hrs. The main force started a frontal attack on the airfield, with the 5th Company conducting an envelopment and the 7th Company (reinforced) a turning movement to the south of Dilly. Lieutenant-Colonel Van Straten reinforced the airfield defences. His retreat route was, however, threatened. Some of the NEI troops had fled. In addition, he could not call in the 2nd Independent Company because of a breakdown in communications. The Australians would not learn of the Japanese landing until around 0900hrs. On seeing the Japanese fleet, Van Straten estimated the Japanese strength to be 4,000–5,000 men. At around 0800hrs, he decided to make a general retreat towards 2nd Independent Company. By the end of the morning, Dilly was in Japanese hands.

The IJA's losses amounted to seven killed. On the Allied side, 24 soldiers lost their lives: eight NEI men and 16 Australians. The number of Allied prisoners of war was 33.

The defeated Australian and NEI troops from Dutch and Portuguese Timor retreated into the mountains. They eventually started a guerrilla campaign. However, that story is beyond the scope of this book.

With the capture of Timor, and the Carrier Task Force in the waters south of Java, the island's encirclement was complete. It was now cut off from reinforcements from Australia. Within a week, Japanese troops would land on Java.

# JAVA (OPERATION *H*)

On 19 February 1942, on Wavell's advice, the Combined Chiefs of Staff decided to stop sending ground troops to Java as reinforcements. These would be sent to Australia and Burma instead. The Australian army corps on its way to Java was therefore no longer to be shipped to Java. The island was thus, to all intents and purposes, given up. Wavell resigned as Supreme Commander, closed his personal headquarters and left Java on 25 February 1942. Dutch officers took command. Lieutenant-General H. ter Poorten, already the commander ABDA-ARM, also became the commander-in-chief for the ABDA area. On Java, ABDA-AIR was renamed Java Air Command (JAC) with Major-General L.H. van Oijen at its head. Vice Admiral C.E.L. Helfrich was from 14 February the commander of ABDA-FLOAT.

# Operation *H*: the conquest of Java

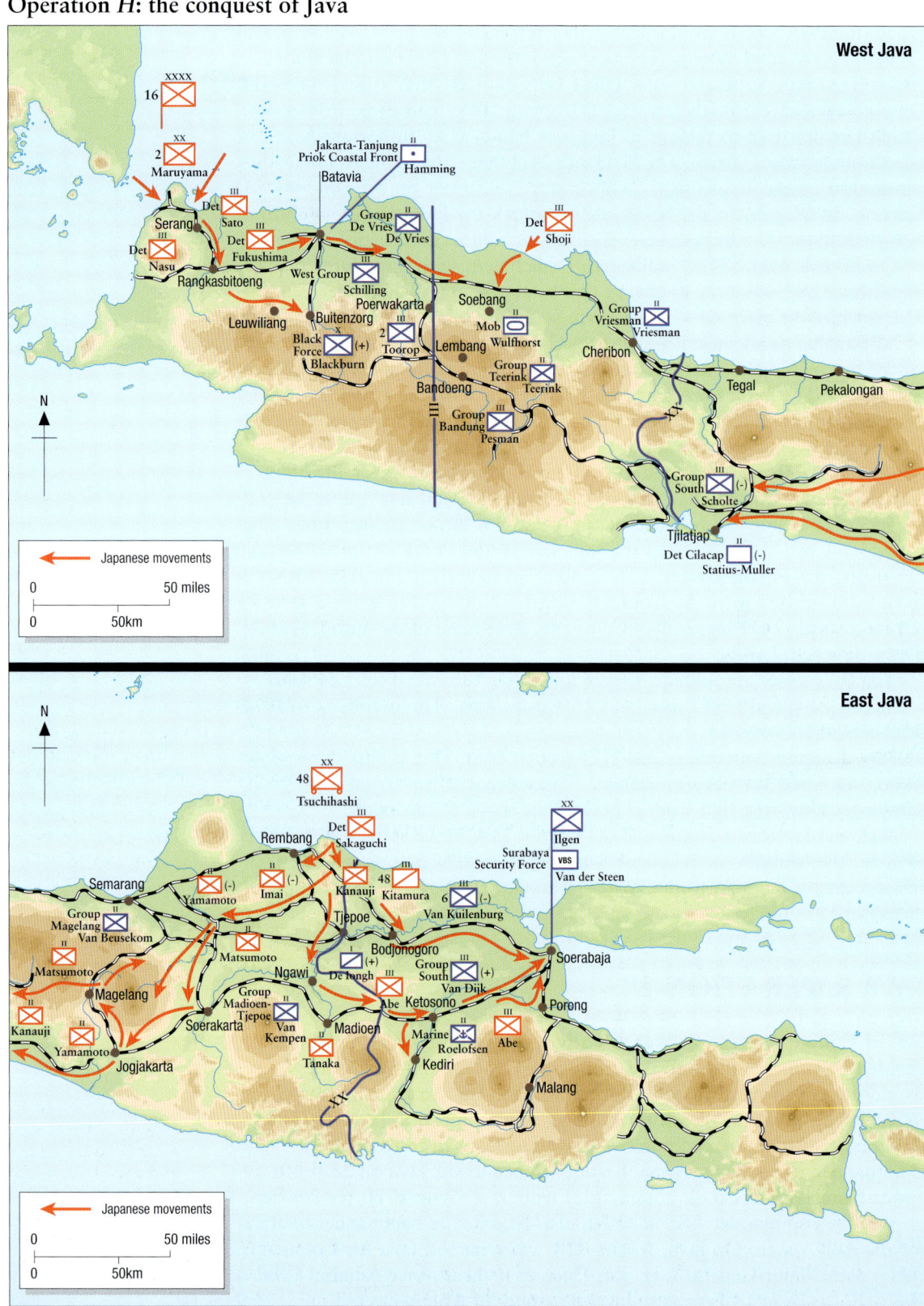

On 22 February 1942, the RNEI General HQ decided to adjust the operation plan for Java in the absence of further Allied support. This was a week before the Japanese landings on Java. In order to achieve some success against the expected superior numbers of Japanese troops, it was decided to concentrate on West Java with the simultaneous formation of a strategic reserve. The transfer of troops from East Java was vetoed by order of the governor general. The Commander of the Navy found the Surabaya fleet base indispensable for supporting the navy. Central Java, however, was abandoned. With the 3rd Division in East Java, a certain fragmentation of forces remained.

The decision had repercussions on command lines and troop positions in West and Central Java. In West Java, the area of operations of 1st Division was reorganized into separate commands: West Group, Bandung Group and East Group. A separate East Group command was ultimately not instituted. West Group, Bandung Group and 3rd Division (East Java) consisted of an infantry regiment with support weapons. The 2nd Infantry Regiment became the strategic reserve for West Java with the 1st Mountain Artillery Battalion. To comply with these changes in the operational plan, the necessary troops were moved from Central to West Java to their new and mostly unfamiliar operating areas. They did not have time to settle in there, because the Japanese ground offensive in Java had now erupted in all its intensity.

The air offensive against Java was carried out in East Java by the IJN 11th Air Fleet and in West Java by the IJA with the Third Air Force and the IJN 11th Air Fleet. The IJN and IJA faced a shortage of suitable air bases and logistical problems. In addition, the IJN's air operations were severely affected by bad weather. The preparatory air offensive against Java had begun on 3 February 1942 with Operation Z, a three-day air offensive to eliminate Allied airpower in East Java. The targets were Surabaya, Madioen and Malang. After two days of action, 3 and 5 February 1942, the IJN was convinced that Allied airpower in East Java had been virtually eliminated. New attacks followed on 7, 8 and 9 February. Due to bad weather, the next attack did not take place until 18 February 1942. The weather also interfered with IJN air operations against West Java, and the focus was shifted to attack Allied shipping around Bangka. The IJA was only able to start its air campaign against West Java on 19 February from Palembang. When the Western Landing Unit departed on 18 February, the air offensive against Java had yet to begin. There was no question of air superiority over Java. In the eyes of the IJN, the air offensive against West Java did not bear enough fruit. The Allied naval and air forces remained active. For this reason, the IJN proposed postponing the landing on Java by two days until 28 February 1942. The Southern Task Force was reinforced and the air campaign against West Java intensified.

During Operation Z, the IJN air units by chance also engaged the Allied naval Striking Force. It was thought that heavy losses had been inflicted on the Allied ships during two days of air attacks. In fact, only two American cruisers were damaged; aboard the USS *Houston*, 48 men died and 20 were injured.

ABDA-AIR responded to the loss of South Sumatra with an offensive counter-air operation aimed at impairing Japanese flight capacity as far as possible by bombing attacks on the oil tank farm at Plaju Refinery, shipping on the Musi River, the Muntok anchorage and Palembang I Airfield. This

**OPPOSITE**
Java was the main island and administrative centre of the Netherlands East Indies. It was a long (c. 1,060km) and narrow (200km) island with a population of about 42 million. A mountainous volcanic area extends the length of the island. The north coast consists of lowland terrain with many rivers flowing down from the mountains. The south coast terrain, on the other hand, is frequently mountainous. Any primary forest had largely been cleared. The Priangan is a high plateau in West Java, containing the city of Bandung (Bandoeng), surrounded by middle and high mountains. The island had three modern ports: Tanjung Priok (West Java), Surabaya (East Java) and Cilacap (Tjilatjap, on the south coast in Central Java). The road network was well developed with metalled west–east connecting roads and railways along the north and south coasts. At Cepu (Tjepoe) in Central Java there was an oil refinery.

*The amphibious landing of the Sato Detachment in Area No. 1, Sector C, Bantam Bay near St Nicholas Point. Sectors A and B were north and south of Merak on the Sunda Strait. The Japanese prepared amphibious landings to take place in complete darkness and carried them out after moonrise, preferably on days when the tide was highest at daybreak. On Tarakan, the landing was on a half-ebb tide. They used special landing craft. The unloading was done by troops. Bantam Bay turned out to be inappropriate for unloading. After the ships at Merak had finished on 4 March 1942, the transport ships sailed from Bantam Bay to Merak to continue with unloading. (Mainichi Newspapers)*

counter-offensive was partly successful, but proved insufficient to stop the Japanese offensive. FEAF, in turn, carried out an independent offensive counter-air operation against Bali after its fall. In addition to the offensive counter-air action, Allied fighter aircraft, partly in conjunction with anti-aircraft artillery, were deployed in a defensive counter-air operation: the air defence of the airfields, the main ports and the navy. By the end of February 1942, aircraft reinforcements were en route by ship to Java. However, the seaplane tender USS *Langley* was sunk and the aircraft on the MS *Sea Witch* were packed in crates and were yet to be assembled. In the end, there was not enough time for that. Its cargo had to be destroyed.

The Sixteenth Army's operation plan from mid-February 1942 provided for simultaneous landings at dawn on 26 February in West and East Java. The 48th Division landed at Kragan and captured Surabaya. The Sakaguchi Detachment also landed at Kragan and captured Cilacap in Central Java. The 2nd Division landed in Bantam Bay. The primary goal was the conquest of Jakarta. A powerful secondary force advanced to Bogor to capture this city. The Shoji Detachment landed at Eretan Wetan, captured Kalidjati Airfield by surprise and occupied the bridge over the Citarum River to block the road between Jakarta and Bandung. After the capture of Jakarta, the main body of the 2nd Division and the Shoji Detachment were to jointly attack the Bandung stronghold from the north. Bandung was therefore the secondary goal. Depending on the circumstances, the ancillary forces from Bogor and the Shoji Detachment would occupy Bandung in one go. In February 1942, Southern Army considered deploying the 1st Raiding Group to take Cilacap. This would cut off the return and supply route on Java. In the end, this was cancelled.

On 26 February 1942, the two Japanese invasion fleets approached Java Island from the bases at Cam Ranh Bay and Jolo. The Western Landing Unit comprised 56 transport ships and 27 warships. The Eastern Landing Unit counted 38 transport ships for the 48th Division and two for the Sakaguchi Detachment. This unit was spotted on 25 February 1942 at the Balikpapan anchorage. The Allied Combined Striking Force sailed from Surabaya to search for and attack the Eastern Transport Fleet. The transport ships were not found. However, the squadron did encounter the Japanese escort unit. The resulting Battle of the Java Sea followed on 27 and 28 February 1942, with the Combined Striking Force finally defeated. With this success, the IJN controlled the waters around Java. The invasion was postponed for just one day.

On the night of Saturday 28 February to Sunday 1 March 1942, the Sixteenth Army conducted amphibious landings on the Java coast. Operation *H* had begun. The Western Landing Unit came ashore at two landing zones in West Java. The Sixteenth Army HQ and the 2nd Division landed in Area No. 1 with the main force in the Bay of Bantam from 0030hrs and a detachment at Merak from 0200hrs. The Shoji Detachment landed in Area No. 2 about 200km east at Eretan Wetan. The Eastern Assault Force, consisting of the 48th Division and the Sakaguchi Detachment, landed near Kragan in East Java.

The landing zones were far apart. This meant that the Java campaign would consist of widely separated operational areas. This made it difficult for the Sixteenth Army to direct the troops in Central and East Java in particular. To allow these troops to operate independently, special units and equipment were added, clear operational instructions were provided, and a special staff officer was posted to the headquarters. This control problem was exacerbated by the loss of Sixteenth Army communications equipment and codebooks upon landing. Without his means of communication, General Imamura lacked command and control over his Sixteenth Army during the campaign in Java.

The defenders' intelligence position on Java was unequivocally terrible. On 1 March 1942, it was estimated that the Japanese had landed two to three divisions in West Java. At least two divisions would have landed at Kragan. On 4 March 1942, this number was adjusted upwards: four in Bantam, one near Indramayu (Eretan Wetan) and in East Java probably between two and four divisions. In fact, the Java Army and the Sixteenth Army were numerically about the same strength, as indicated in Table 10.[14]

**Table 10: Troop strengths**

| Area | Japanese Sixteenth Army | RNEI Army | Allies |
|---|---|---|---|
| West Group | 20,500 | 17,500 | 3,400 |
| Bandung Group | 3,000 | 5,900 | |
| Central Java | 4,000 | 9,000 | |
| East Java | 20,000 | 17,300 | |
| **Total** | **47,500** | **49,700** | **3,400** |

## West Java

During the landing in Bantam Bay, the Japanese ships were fired upon by the Allied ships USS *Houston* and HMAS *Perth*, who wanted to escape to the west. In the following confusing battle, both ships were sunk. A Japanese transport ship was sunk by friendly fire and three transport ships were severely damaged, ran aground and heeled over. Nor were the Japanese spared from air strikes. Between 27 February and 1 March 1942, Allied air forces switched from counter-air against the Palembang area to harassing attacks on Japanese landing operations. The transport fleets, the landings themselves and the disembarkation of supplies were bombed and strafed.

At Merak the small NEI coastal detachment (*c.* 40 men) opposed the landing, but was soon forced to retreat. The Nasu Detachment that landed at Merak consisted of the 16th Infantry Regiment (reduced) and 2nd Reconnaissance Regiment. This detachment had to carry out the supporting attack towards Bogor. With the motorized 2nd Reconnaissance Regiment, a unit of battalion strength, in the vanguard, Serang was occupied that same morning at 0700hrs.

Throughout their offensive in the NEI, the Japanese made extensive use of tanks, although they were not as decisive on the battlefield as at Malacca. At the front of this mechanized and motorized column on the road to Serang, West Java, we see two light tanks of the battalion-size 2nd Tank Regiment. There are no civilians looking on. The tanks are Type 95 Ha-Go light tanks, armed with a Type 94 (1934) 37mm gun in the turret and 7.7mm Type 97 MG in the front hull. The tank commander can be seen in the turret. Instead of a tank helmet, he wears his fieldcap backwards. A wooden frame has been added to the tank, to attach camouflage material, as shown on the second tank that follows. (Mainichi Newspapers)

14 Auxiliary troops are not included in the Dutch figures.

Kalidjati Airfield was one of the main Military Aviation Service operating bases. In February 1942, ABDA-AIR allocated two squadrons to Kalidjati: No. 84 (Bomber) Squadron RAF and No. 1 (General Reconnaissance) Squadron RAAF. The Dutch 1st Aircraft Group also operated from the airfield. Ground-based air defence was provided by 49th Battery, 48th Light Anti-Aircraft Regiment (RA) and units from 3rd Anti-Aircraft Battalion. On the morning of the Japanese landing, the RNEI Army 3rd Company, 2nd Infantry Battalion was relieved by 12th Battery, 6th Heavy Anti-Aircraft Regiment (RA) deployed in a ground-defence roll. The Australian and NEI air units managed to evacuate the airfield in time. The British, however, were too slow. This photo of the airfield was taken between 1930 and 1932. By 1942, the airfield had been extended to include two runways west of the lake at the bottom of the picture. To the right lies the road to Subang, the direction from which the Japanese approached the airfield. (Leiden University Libraries, KITLV 49427)

The city was an important crossroads. The unit turned south and took Rangkasbitoeng by surprise at 1230hrs. The NEI detachment at Rangkasbitoeng, consisting of 10th Battalion, 2nd Infantry Regiment, 1st Mountain Artillery Battalion and two armoured cars, failed. It hastily retreated, with little of the intended delaying actions coming to pass. The Fukushima Detachment also landed at Merak. It was made up of the 4th Infantry Regiment (reduced). It took the bridge and lock at Pamarajan over the Ciujung River by surprise. The Sato Detachment, consisting of the reinforced 29th Infantry Regiment, landed in Bantam Bay. Together with the Fukushima Detachment, the Sato Detachment formed the main force with Jakarta as its objective. However, Sato's advance along the northern route progressed very slowly due to felled trees blocking the road and destroyed bridges. Deep rivers and high banks in combination with swollen rivers after heavy rainfall made bridge restoration difficult. The detachment did not reach the Ciujung River until 3 March 1942.

For West Group's commander, Major-General Schilling, the landings in Bantam Bay certainly came as no surprise. However, the Japanese advance along the southern route was considerably faster than expected. The two roads from Serang to Jakarta and Bogor diverged. An advance along both routes would only increase the distance between the enemy axes of advance. The rapid Japanese southern advance further increased the distance. According to Schilling, this offered an opportunity to achieve a limited success. He decided to concentrate his force against this southern axis of advance. However, because of developments at Kalidjati, he had to cancel his counter-attack.

The Shoji Detachment was landed from seven transport ships under cover of a light cruiser and four destroyers at Eretan Wetan between 0330 and 0430hrs on 1 March 1942. Instead of using infantry to secure the beachhead, Shoji immediately put the tanks and trucks ashore. The Wakamatsu Raiding Unit – 2nd Battalion, 230th Infantry Regiment with the 1st Company, 4th Tank Regiment (less elements, comprising ten Type 95 Ha-Go light tanks) and with the transport company attached – landed and immediately rushed towards Kalidjati. The Egashira Raiding Unit (1st Battalion, 230th Infantry Regiment) was assigned the seizure of the bridge over the Citarum River. The Ono Unit had to secure the landing zone and served as a reserve for the detachment. Even before landing, Allied planes attacked the convoy, but without success. In the morning, more air raids followed on the landing beach and on the ships. The Japanese losses amounted to about 100 men. The air cover, in the form of four seaplanes from the auxiliary seaplane tenders *Sanyo Maru* and *Kamikawa Maru*, was driven off.

En route to the airfield, Wakamatsu dealt with several small NEI Country Guards surveillance detachments, Home Guard troops and an improvised roadblock east of Kalidjati manned by a regular infantry platoon. The way was clear. The airfield garrison at Kalidjati was caught off-guard. That same morning, the ground defence had been taken over by 12th Battery, 6th Heavy

Anti-Aircraft Regiment. This unit had lost its anti-aircraft guns in South Sumatra and was deployed as infantry for airfield defence. By 1230hrs, the intact airfield was in Japanese hands. In addition, of the remaining RAF and RAAF bomber fleet of 33 aircraft, 26 (including the last eight serviceable Blenheims) were lost. The airfield had been kept operational for as long as possible. On 28 February 1942, Java Air Command took evacuation and destruction measures. However, these were not yet implemented.

Kalidjati Airfield was located in the coastal plain at the foot of the Priangan, only 40km from the Bandung army base. If this operational airfield fell into Japanese hands, it would pose a very serious threat. The RNEI General Headquarters decided to concentrate its forces against the isolated and scattered Shoji Detachment. The operational plan provided for the reconquest of Subang and Kalidjati by deploying the strategic reserve (2nd Infantry Regiment and 1st Mountain Artillery Battalion) from the south-west on 3 March 1942. On 2 March, a reconnaissance in force by three infantry-heavy teams was ordered against the Japanese beachhead. Each team included an infantry battalion and an artillery battery, and two of the teams also had a squadron of motorized cavalry. The next day, these teams (De Vries Group, Teerink Group and Vriesman Group) had to support the main attack.

On 1 March 1942, Java Air Command deployed the remaining Military Aviation Service and RAF aircraft against the transport ships and the landing site at Eretan Wetan, and from 2 March also against captured Kalidjati to delay the operational launch as much as possible. On 1 March, fighter aircraft also strafed Japanese columns inland. They were relatively successful in this. On 28 February, 29 bombers, 22 fighters and ten reconnaissance aircraft were available exclusively for Reconnaissance Group and East Group.

The Mobile Unit (*Mobiele Eenheid*), a tank and armoured infantry company, was transferred to Bandung Group. Major-General Pesman was convinced that the airfield was only occupied by a small Japanese advance guard. He ordered the Mobile Unit to retake Kalidjati Airfield. Follow-on forces would then hold the airfield. On 2 March, in the morning, the Mobile Unit (under Captain G.J. Wulfhorst), reinforced with the 2nd Battery, 2nd Mountain Artillery Battalion, attacked Subang. In the town was the HQ of the Shoji Detachment protected by an infantry company. Although the Japanese were taken completely by surprise, the Mobile Unit failed to break through to the airfield and had to withdraw with heavy losses of men and materiel. During the retreat, it converged with Teerink Group, a battalion-size unit reinforced with 1st Battery, 2nd Mountain Artillery Battalion. Captain Wulfhorst and Major Teerink, however, were not aware of each

**ABOVE LEFT**
A Vickers-Carden-Loyd Light Tank Model 1936. This two-man tank weighed 3.8 tons, had a maximum armour thickness of 9mm and was armed with a Vickers .303 machine gun in the turret. This photo dates from before the NEI mobilization. After the outbreak of war, an orange triangle with a black border was painted on the turret, pointing downwards. On the side, the unit code 'QC' (15cm tall) of the NEI Mobile Unit was applied in white paint. (Netherlands Institute of Military History)

**ABOVE RIGHT**
A platoon of seven newly arrived Marmon-Herrington CTLS-4TA tanks was assigned to the Mobile Unit. The two-man 7.2-ton tank proved unsuccessful. The turret, which mounted a .30-cal. Browning M1919 machine gun, could only rotate 270 degrees. Its armour was not resistant to machine-gun fire and the tracks were unreliable. Radios were not yet installed. The first three tanks in the photo are CTLS-4TAY variants with the turret on the left. The following tanks are CTLS-4TAC variants with the turret on the right. Most of the new tanks were not ready in time for the NEI campaign, and some were shipped to the Dutch colony of Surinam. This photo was taken there in 1942. (Museum Bronbeek)

Brigadier Blackburn formed a brigade on 21 and 22 February 1942 from Australian units and troops on Java: Blackforce. This force was only equipped with small arms. It could, however, be supplied from stores diverted from Singapore to Batavia. These included vehicles, some MG carriers and a 'considerable number' of light armoured cars. Blackforce was first used for the protection of five airfields. On 27 February 1942, the force was relocated and concentrated on the Tjampea tea plantation outside Bogor. It moved on 2 March 1942 to Leuwiliang to counter the advancing Japanese. (Australian War Memorial)

other's positions. A golden opportunity was lost due to a lack of coordination and communication. The three teams tasked with the reconnaissance in force probed the beachhead as ordered.

The Japanese also suffered from communication problems. The 3rd Air Division did not begin operations over Kalidjati with most of the 27th Air Group until the afternoon of 2 March 1942. It flew air defence over Kalidjati and launched attacks against Andir Airfield at Bandung. Lieutenant-General Imamura did not hear of the capture of Kalidjati until 4 March.

The battle in West Java on the southern axis was quite different. At Leuwiliang, the rapid advance of the Nasu Detachment was halted. There, a company support position was built by the Dutch on the eastern bank of the Cianten River. In the early hours of 2 or 3 March 1942, this was occupied by the Australian Blackforce under Brigadier A.S. Blackburn. After cancelling the planned counter-attack in West Java, Blackforce was tasked with defending the Bogor area. Based on information about Japanese tactics in Malaya, Blackburn organized his defence in depth. One company occupied the fortified position, with a second company held in reserve. Blackburn kept the main force back as a mobile reserve.

The first troops in contact in Leuwiliang comprised the advanced guard of the Nasu Detachment, the 2nd Reconnaissance Regiment under Lieutenant-Colonel Kinichi Noguchi, at 1330hrs on 3 March 1942. Several attempts to cross the Cianten River further southwards and attack Blackforce in the flank failed. After midnight on 4 March, Major-General Yumio Nasu, commander of 2nd Division infantry group and the Nasu Detachment, took control of the battle. While the 2nd Reconnaisance Regiment contained Blackforce to the front, the 3rd Battalion, 16th Infantry Regiment crossed the swollen river 3km to the south with the regimental gun and anti-tank gun companies in support. The 2nd Battalion followed in reserve. However, this envelopment was blocked east of the river by a determined company from 2nd Battalion, Blackforce.

The reinforced 2nd Infantry Regiment under Colonel C.G. Toorop launched the delayed major counter-attack on 3 March 1942 at around 1000hrs. The advance to contact took place in a battle formation over open ground and over more than 10km on foot. At 0715hrs, an armoured car platoon of 1st Cavalry Squadron made it to the airfield, probably by mistake. The advance route was not blocked and free of Japanese outposts. The element of surprise was, however, lost due to reconnaissance by aircraft and the premature appearance of the vanguard of 1st Cavalry Squadron. Air support was not available, because the main Andir Airfield at Bandung was temporarily put out of action after a major Japanese air attack in the morning. From 1300 to 1730hrs, the 2nd Infantry Regiment was subject to repeated air strikes involving bombers and fighter aircraft from the 3rd Air Division from Kalidjati. Not only did the advance come to a halt, but the 2nd Infantry Regiment was also dispersed and thrown back in confusion. Its morale was broken. The flank attack of Group Teerink south of Subang was also spotted and suffered a similar fate. The major counter-attack of the RNEI Army had thus ended in catastrophe. An attack on the landing site at Eretan Wetan by Vriesman Group was also repelled by the Japanese with the support of naval gun fire.

The Sixteenth Army indentified Jakarta as its operational target and remained prepared for a NEI counter-offensive in West Java. On 3 and 4 March 1942, it became clear that the NEI troops in West Java had adopted a defensive attitude. Conversely, they made an offensive stand against the Shoji Detachment. The Sixteenth Army was concerned about the predicament of the Shoji Detachment. On 4 March, it asked the Southern Army to reinforce the Shoji Detachment with two companies flown in from Palembang to Kalidjati. This request was denied. The Sixteenth Army then decided to shift the centre of gravity of the 2nd Division to the southern axis of advance. The Fukushima Detachment was shifted to the southern route and the Nasu Detachment received reinforcements from the Sato Detachment. The aim was to quickly force a breakthrough at Leuwiliang and then attack Bandung via Bogor to support the Shoji Detachment.

The RNEI Army had used up its strategic reserve in the failed major counter-attack against the Shoji Detachment. There was no longer any question of further large-scale offensive operations. The RNEI General Headquarters therefore decided on 4 March to focus on the defence of the Bandung plateau. West Group was ordered to withdraw to the plateau as soon as possible. The retreat and preparation would certainly take several days. In the meantime, Bandung Group had to defend the entrances to the plateau on its own. The remaining Allied air forces were made available to the Bandung Group. West Group retreated from the vicinity of Jakarta via Bogor by road and rail to Bandung, covered by Blackforce holding out at Leuwiliang. Blackburn withdrew on 5 March 1942. His losses were *c.* 150 men.

Colonel Shoji estimated the strength of the RNEI Army troops around Bandung at first to be between 30,000 and 35,000. At Subang he had narrowly escaped a heavy blow. He feared that his widely deployed detachment would be surrounded and destroyed. Therefore, he wanted to seize and hold a position on the high ground. After repulsing the counter-attacks of 2 and 3 March, Colonel Shoji changed his mind on 4 March after reassessing the military situation. He decided, in contradiction to Imamura's orders, to

**ABOVE LEFT**
On 3 March 1942, the IJA 3rd Air Division bombed and strafed the attacking columns of the NEI 2nd Infantry Regiment (reinforced) for four hours in six missions with 27 aircraft. The NEI infantry had left the vehicles east of Sadang on the Sadang–Kalidjati–Subang road around 1000hrs and advanced through the terrain. The disembarked troops and vehicles were continuously bombed from the air in the afternoon. This meant the end of any hope of recapturing Kalidjati Airfield. This grainy photograph was probably taken on the aforementioned road. Two trucks and a bus can be made out among the wreckage, along with a Japanese soldier at centre. (Public domain)

**ABOVE RIGHT**
A Japanese war painting by Kenji Yoshioka, 'Bombing West Area of Kalidjati Airfield, Java'. The scene shows destroyed vehicles and abandoned weapons of the RNEI Army's 2nd Infantry Regiment (reinforced) after the bombing by the 3rd Air Division on 3 March 1942. Fallen soldiers lie between the wreckage. The destroyed materiel is still smoking in the background. Two Japanese planes, probably twin-engine Mitsubishi Ki-51 Army 99 attack aircraft, are circling in the sky. (NARA, public domain)

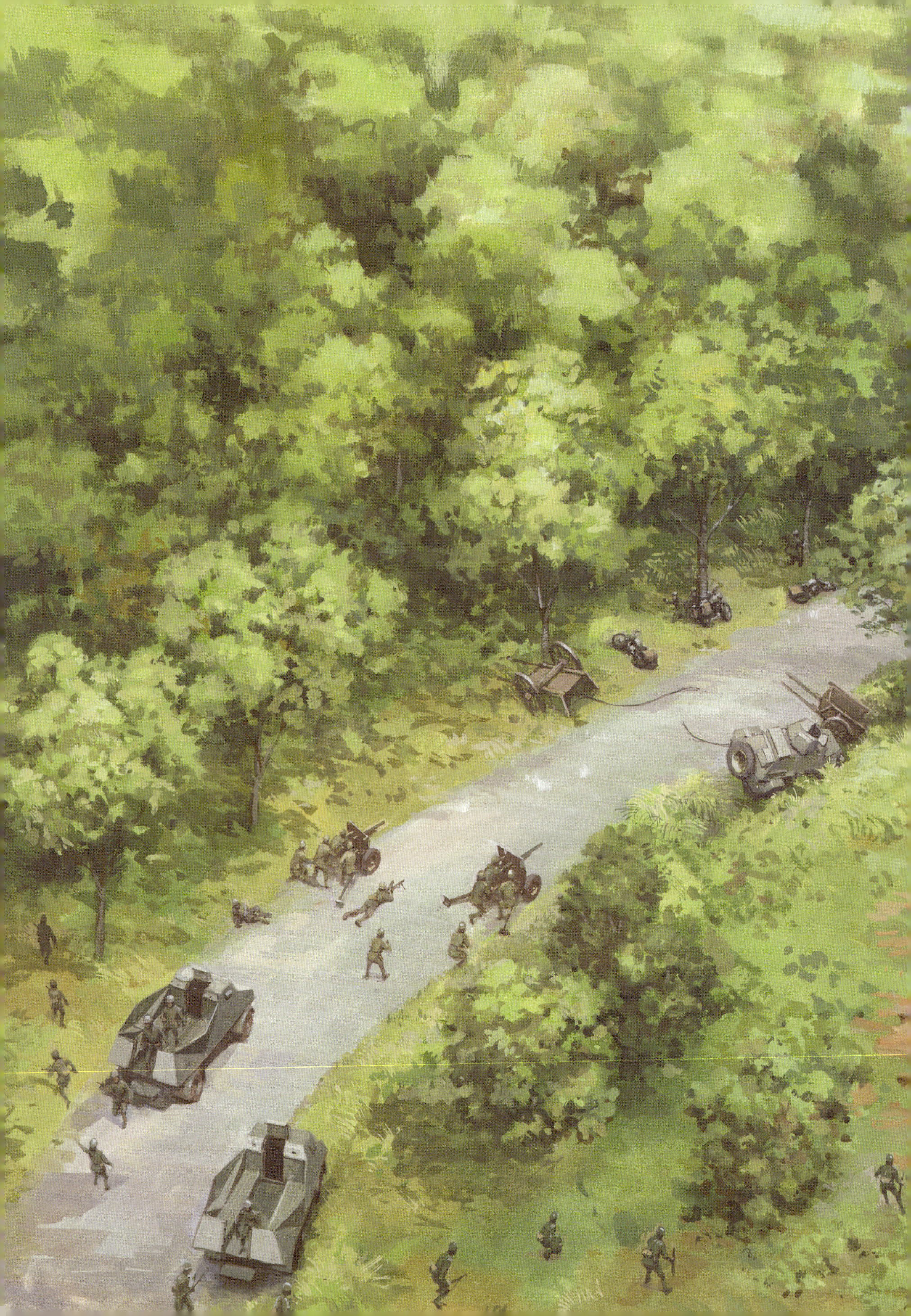

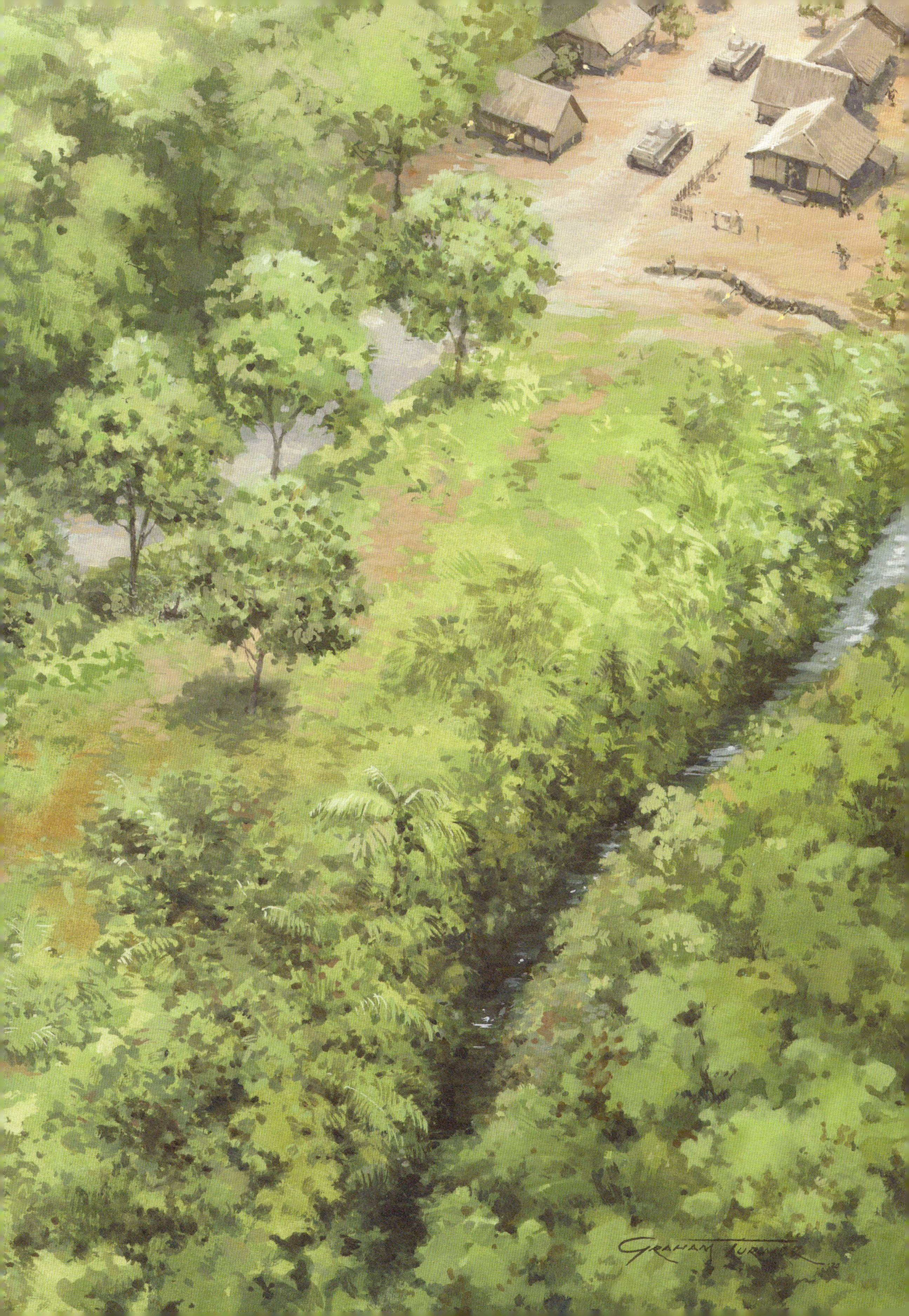
Graham Turner

**THE NEI MOBILE UNIT ATTACKS INTO SUBANG, 2 MARCH 1942 (PP. 78–79)**

On the first day of the Japanese landing on Java, the Shoji Detachment captured Kalidjati Airfield. The RNEI Army responded with various counter-attacks, one of which was by a team of tanks and armoured infantry with artillery support. The Shoji Detachment was widely dispersed with its HQ at Subang, its 2nd Battalion (reduced) and airfield units at Kalidjati, 1st Battalion (reduced) to the north and 6th Company securing its landing site. At Subang, Colonel Shoji's HQ was secured by 4th Company, 1st Battalion (100 men in total) equipped with a mountain gun, an anti-tank gun and two MGs.

On Monday 2 March 1942, at 0810hrs (Java Time), the NEI Mobile Unit, commanded by Captain G.J. Wulfhorst, attacked Subang. It was made up of its HQ, a reconnaissance section, a tank company, an armoured infantry company, one AT gun section and a supply train. It was reinforced with the 2nd Battery, 2nd Mountain Artillery Battalion. What followed was the first tank attack in Dutch military history.

This scene show the moments after the attacking NEI armoured column forced its way through a road obstacle just south of Subang, and became pinned down in a firefight with Japanese defenders. We see a broken steel-wire cable (**1**) emplaced by the Japanese to block the road, hidden by two (now pushed aside) carts (**2**). The Dutch Marmon Herrington armoured car Mk III that broke the cable lies overturned on the right of the road (**3**). The lead NEI tank platoon (comprising seven Marmon Herrington CTLS-4TA tanks) has advanced in single file (**4**) up the road and is pushing on towards Subang. On either side of the road, Japanese troops have taken up positions in civilian-built air-raid trenches, ditches, inside the houses and behind trees (**5**). They have opened fire on the following NEI infantry as they disembark from the APCs (**6**). The Ambonese 1st Platoon infantry are moving into the rubber plantation to the left of the road (**7**), while the Menadonese 2nd Platoon are deploying to the right (**8**). The company commander is standing in the road with a LMG gunner lying prone alongside him (**9**). A Japanese LMG gunner, in a forward position camouflaged with a net has suffered a firing malfunction (**10**). The two NEI AT guns have taken up position on the road (**11**).

Although the Japanese were taken completely by surprise, the Mobile Unit failed to exploit this tactical success. The terrain prevented deployment and the tanks had to fight in a single file in a built-up area. The armoured infantry company, pinned down in the fire fight south of Subang, could not follow the tanks. Without infantry support, a dash towards the airfield was meaningless. The tank platoon turned and forced its way back through.

To get the NEI infantry further into Subang, a second attack by another tank platoon was mounted at 0915hrs. At 1000hrs, the Japanese threatened the right and left flanks of the infantry. A third NEI tank attack was launched, allowing the NEI infantry to break off the fight and retreat. The Mobile Unit withdrew. The engagement, which lasted for almost two hours, was over.

The Mobile Unit had suffered heavy casualties: 15 killed and 13 wounded (one of whom died later). Materiel losses included 13 tanks, an armoured car, three APCs and one anti-tank gun. During the assault, the unit did not receive fire support. Japanese losses were 20 killed and an unknown number of wounded.

abandon his defensive posture, and shift to the offensive and a full-scale attack to take Bandung. Shoji received full backing from Major-General Endo, commander of 3rd Air Division. Endo moved the centre of gravity of his 3rd Air Division's air support to the Shoji Detachment. He had arrived from Palembang with the 59th and 75th Air groups on 2 March 1942.

The Ciater defensive position (*Tjaterstelling*) guarded the access road from Subang to the Priangan Plateau. The position was built for a regiment in the middle of a tea plantation. It was to be replaced by a new position higher up the mountain and was greatly neglected. The fields of fire were poor, and numerous footbridges had been placed over the wire fence and trenches. The position was guarded until February by a Home Guard brigade (15 men), police and the crew of a 5cm naval gun. On 26/27 February 1942, the (European) 2nd Company, 1st Infantry Battalion (reinforced) arrived. On 1 March, the 3rd Battery, 2nd Mountain Artillery Battalion followed. With these troops, however, only part of the position could be occupied. The Subang–Bandung road passed straight through the position. On the morning of 5 March, the Left-Half 21st Infantry Battalion arrived from Central Java. However, this battalion remained about 2km behind the front. Only around 1800hrs did this unit move into position directly behind the Ciater position.

Shoji assigned the three companies of Wakamatsu's 2nd Battalion, the 1st Company, 4th Tank Regiment and two batteries of mountain artillery for the attack on the position in the Ciater Pass. The Egashira Unit, delayed by NEI destruction and resistance, had finally reached the Citarum River, but found the bridge destroyed. Shoji recalled the unit to Subang. Wakamatsu launched his assault around 1600hrs in the afternoon of Thursday, 5 March 1942. Wakamatsu deployed his battalion and, using the terrain, the vegetation, ground fog and a brief heavy rain shower, a number of pillboxes were taken in the first and second line. He decided to spend the night on the battlefield and continue the attack the next day. According to Shoji, only the outposts had been captured and the main line of resistance on the ridge still had to be taken. On the morning of 6 March, it became clear to Wakamatsu that he had already broken through the main defences.

In the afternoon of 5 March, Colonel W.J. de Veer, commanding officer of 4th Infantry Regiment, was put in charge of the troops at the Ciater position. De Veer organized a defence in depth during the night of 5/6 March 1942, reinforcements feeding in slowly behind the Ciater position. He placed the (Javanese) 2nd Company, 2nd Infantry Battalion and (European) 1st Company, 5th Infantry Battalion behind barbed-wire fences in holes and ditches to the left, and the Left-Half 21st Infantry Battalion to the right of the Subang–Bandung road directly behind the Ciater position. A second line was formed with the Paardekooper Detachment (comprising cadets and reserve officer candidates) in the Wates position under construction. The third line was an all-round defence at the three-way Tolhek crossroads by the Siahaya Detachment (Ambonese recruits). The 3rd Battery, 2nd Mountain Artillery Battalion received reinforcement from the 2nd Battery. Despite

The Japanese 2nd Division's infantry regiments were standardly equipped with bicycles for one-third of its companies. Due to the destroyed roads, bicycles proved to be the ideal means of transport. These Japanese troops are on their way to Jakarta. According to the Japanese *Mainichi* newspaper, enthusiastic Indonesians watch from the roadside. Imamura in part attributed the defeat of the NEI to 'the defection of the indigenous people from the Dutch side'. (Mainichi Newspapers)

**ABOVE LEFT**
In 1940, a position for a regimental-size unit was built in the Ciater Pass on the Subang–Bandung road. The position was located in a tea plantation. An anti-tank obstacle of logs and rails covered by a 5cm naval gun in a pillbox with trenches formed the outpost line. Behind a bridge over a ravine, higher up the slope, lay two lines of pillboxes connected by trenches. The position was originally abandoned and neglected, but was occupied and defended in 1941/42. This grainy photo shows one of the Ciater pillboxes; note the heavily sloping and overgrown terrain, and the limited field of fire. (Public domain)

**ABOVE RIGHT**
A 7.5cm mountain gun (*Bergartillerie*) in position in a bamboo bush. This gun still has metal wheels, while most pieces were converted to pneumatic rubber tyres. The guns were loaded onto a truck for transport. Two batteries of four guns each saw action at the Ciater Pass. The guns were used as infantry support weapons. Artillery battalion batteries were allocated to infantry units. However, at the Ciater Pass, the NEI infantry company commander said that he needed infantry, not artillery. (Beeldbank WO2-NIOD)

reinforcements having arrived, the 2nd Company, 1st Infantry Battalion had withdrawn from the position that evening.

On the northern axis of advance, in the 2nd Division area, the Sato Detachment, reduced to just two battalions, entered evacuated Jakarta in the late evening of 5 March 1942. Due to the NEI troops having retreated, it encountered no resistance to the west of Jakarta. The rapid occupation of the capital was something of a surprise to Sixteenth Army. After Blackforce's retreat at Leuwiliang, the main force of the 2nd Division attacked Bogor in a pincer movement. The city fell into Japanese hands on the morning of 6 March 1942. The next target was Bandung.

On the morning of Friday 6 March, Major Wakamatsu launched his attack on the left flank of the makeshift defences. The two companies left of the road were surprised as they were receiving the bread distribution; no outposts had been set. However, the companies quickly recovered and repelled two infantry assaults. The third attack was supported by cannon and machine-gun fire from three Japanese tanks at the Subang–Bandung junction, but this attack was also repulsed. However, the position was threatened with being overrun. The battered companies broke off the fight and retreated to the right. The units were scattered during this retreat. Although not attacked, the entire Left-Half 21st Infantry Battalion, save one platoon, withdrew when the first shots were fired. The Ciater position had been definitively breached. After this success, Wakamatsu did not pursue the retreating Dutch troops, but consolidated his position pending the arrival of Egashira.

During these battles, about 74 NEI soldiers were captured by the Japanese. In the afternoon of 6 March, or the morning of 7 March, almost all these prisoners were executed by the Japanese, with only a handful surviving the massacre.

In the afternoon of 6 March, Colonel De Veer decided to give up the Wates position and concentrate his defence on the three-way crossroads at Tolhek. A major Japanese infantry attack on the triple junction was beaten back with a spoiling attack. Colonel De Veer was killed. In the morning of 7 March 1942, the troops at the Tolhek crossroads received orders to withdraw to Lembang.

North of Lembang, a resistance line was improvised with 9th Infantry Battalion, 15th Infantry Battalion and De Vries Battalion (formed from remnants of 2nd Infantry Regiment). To this were added two West Coast of Sumatra companies, garrison infantry from West Sumatra, and 4th Infantry

A Japanese war painting of a ground attack by IJA Type 99 assault aircraft (Mitsubishi Ki-51), Allied codename Sonia, from 27th Air Group, 3rd Air Division on an NEI motorized column. Airpower was a decisive factor in the Southern Offensive. With attacks on Allied airfields and the breaking of the aerial line of communication between Java and the outside world, Japan had secured air superiority. This dominance was used against Allied ships and ground troops. The nearly constant Japanese air activity with reconnaissance, strafing and bombing paralyzed NEI troop movements and sapped morale. (Netherlands Institute of Military History)

Battalion. On paper it seemed a decent fighting force, but morale was often very low and its combat value was therefore questionable. Moreover, the RNEI Army was showing signs of disintegration. With the breakthrough at the Ciater position, the fight seemed like it was over.

## Central Java

Kragan was an ideal landing point with a 35km-long beach and major connecting roads in the proximity. The vanguard of the Sakaguchi Detachment, the Kanauji Echelon, set foot ashore 6km south-east of Kragan on 1 March 1942 at 0700hrs. The other two units, the Matsumoto and Yamamoto echelons, did not land until the following day. Their transport ship was slow because it had been damaged during the invasion of Bali. The Sakaguchi Detachment (less the Kume Detachment left on Borneo) consisted of the 2nd and 3rd Infantry battalions, 146th Infantry Regiment, two field artillery batteries, an armoured car unit and 2nd Transport Company with 259th Independent Transport Company attached. Sakaguchi's objective was the southern port city of Cilacap, the capture of which would cut off the escape route from Jakarta and Bandung. In the second phase, it would mop up remaining enemy units in Central Java.

The RNEI Army's 2nd Division, based in Central Java, under Major-General P.A. Cox, was reduced on 22 February 1942 by the relocation to West Java of 4th Infantry Regiment. South Group, two motorized cavalry squadrons (4th Cavalry Squadron and Life Guards Cavalry Squadron) and the Cilacap Detachment remained. South Group was a weak infantry regiment formed in January 1942 by merging three understrengh and underarmed infantry battalions and a newly formed machine-gun company of mostly semi-trained Indonesian part-time auxiliary soldiers. The unit was almost fully motorized. South Group was tasked with 'security and protection [of Cilacap port]' by positioning itself behind the Serayu River'.

# JAPANESE BREAKTHROUGH AT CIATER PASS, 5–7 MARCH 1942

After the successful Japanese amphibious landings on the island of Java, Kalidjati Airfield was captured the same morning intact. Repeated NEI counter-attacks were repulsed. On 5 March, the Shoji Detachment attacked the Ciater position from Subang with one infantry battalion and ample air support from the 3rd Air Division. The Ciater position north of the city of Bandung was defended by Group Bandung with a single reinforced infantry company. After the main defensive line was breached, rushed-in NEI reinforcements tried to halt the Japanese advance. Once these forces were also eliminated, the road to Bandung lay open.

## ▼ EVENTS

Times are given in Java Time (JBBT – UTC+07:30) unless otherwise stated.

### Thursday, 5 March 1942

**1.** 1600hrs (JST): Japanese 2nd Battalion, 230th Infantry Regiment (Wakamatsu) consisting of three companies supported by 1st Company, 4th Tank Regiment and two batteries from the 3rd Battalion, 38th Mountain Artillery Regiment advance along the Subang–Lembang road and unexpectedly encounter the Ciater position. The battalion deploys and is ordered to attack. The position on the ridge is defended by the (European) reinforced 2nd Company, 1st Infantry Battalion with 3rd Battery, 2nd Mountain Artillery Battalion in support. Making use of the rugged terrain and the trees hindering the field of fire from the pillboxes, ground mist and a heavy shower, the Japanese manage to break through the position. In the evening, the Japanese advance halts. The troops do not withdraw, but remain overnight in the field.

**2.** 1630hrs: NEI forces conduct reconnaissance using six armoured cars on the Subang–Lembang road. Three armoured cars are put out of action.

**3.** By nightfall, NEI reinforcements arrive, but 2nd Company, 1st Infantry Battalion pulls back. Colonel De Veer, CO 4th Infantry Regiment and in command off the Ciater defence, organizes a defence in-depth. During the night, the Japanese send out patrols.

### Friday, 6 March 1942

**4.** In the early morning, the Japanese infantry suddenly attack the left flank of 2nd Company, 2nd Infantry Battalion and 1st Company, 5th Infantry Battalion. The assault party, followed by a second one, forms directly from the column of march, and is repulsed. The Japanese infantry assault receives support from three tanks firing from the road. The anti-tank rifle group attached to 1st Company, 5th Infantry Battalion has disappeared during the night. At the beginning of the fight, the Left-Half 21st Infantry Battalion is mostly broken and withdraws. A third Japanese attack supported by canon and machine-gun fire from the tanks is stopped with heavy losses. The defenders are forced to retreat. The Ciater position and De Veer's first line is broken. Wakamatsu does not immediately pursue the NEI troops, but consolidates his position. During the day, aircraft of the Japanese 3rd Air Division bomb and strafe the NEI positions and lines of communication.

**5.** Colonel De Veer moves his second line back to the triple junction. At 1700hrs, the long-awaited Japanese attack materializes. De Veer orders a counter-attack, and is killed in action. The Japanese attack is repulsed. An all-round defence at Tolhek is set up. In the afternoon, or early morning of 7 March, the Japanese execute 74 NEI prisoners.

### Saturday, 7 March 1942

**6.** 0200hrs: The defenders at Tolhek commanded by Captain Paardekooper are ordered to withdraw to Lembang.

**7.** Group Bandung orders Lieutenant-Colonel Van Altena to form a new line of defence north of Lembang with three depleted battalions of the 2nd Infantry Regiment, 4th Infantry Battalion and the West Coast of Sumatra Detachment. However, almost all units are showing signs of fatigue and lack cohesion.

**8.** 1300hrs (JST): The Japanese 2nd Battalion (Wakamatsu) starts its advance west of the main road. The advance along a footpath and rough terrain is naturally slow. Using the onset of darkness and persistent rainfall, his advance units attack and surprise the HQ of 9th Infantry Battalion west of Lembang and break up the spread-out NEI battalion. The 3rd Air Division continues its air interdiction missions.

**9.** The Japanese 1st Battalion (Egashira), brought from Krawang by motor transport, follows along the main road slightly after. Around 1600hrs, it probes the spread-out positions of the NEI 4th Infantry Battalion north of Lembang.

**10.** After the first Japanese attack, the NEI 4th Infantry Battalion retreats in an orderly manner towards Bandung. The Japanese 2nd Battalion enters Lembang in the evening. Major-General Pesman, CO Group Bandung, dispatches an officer to negotiate a local surrender.

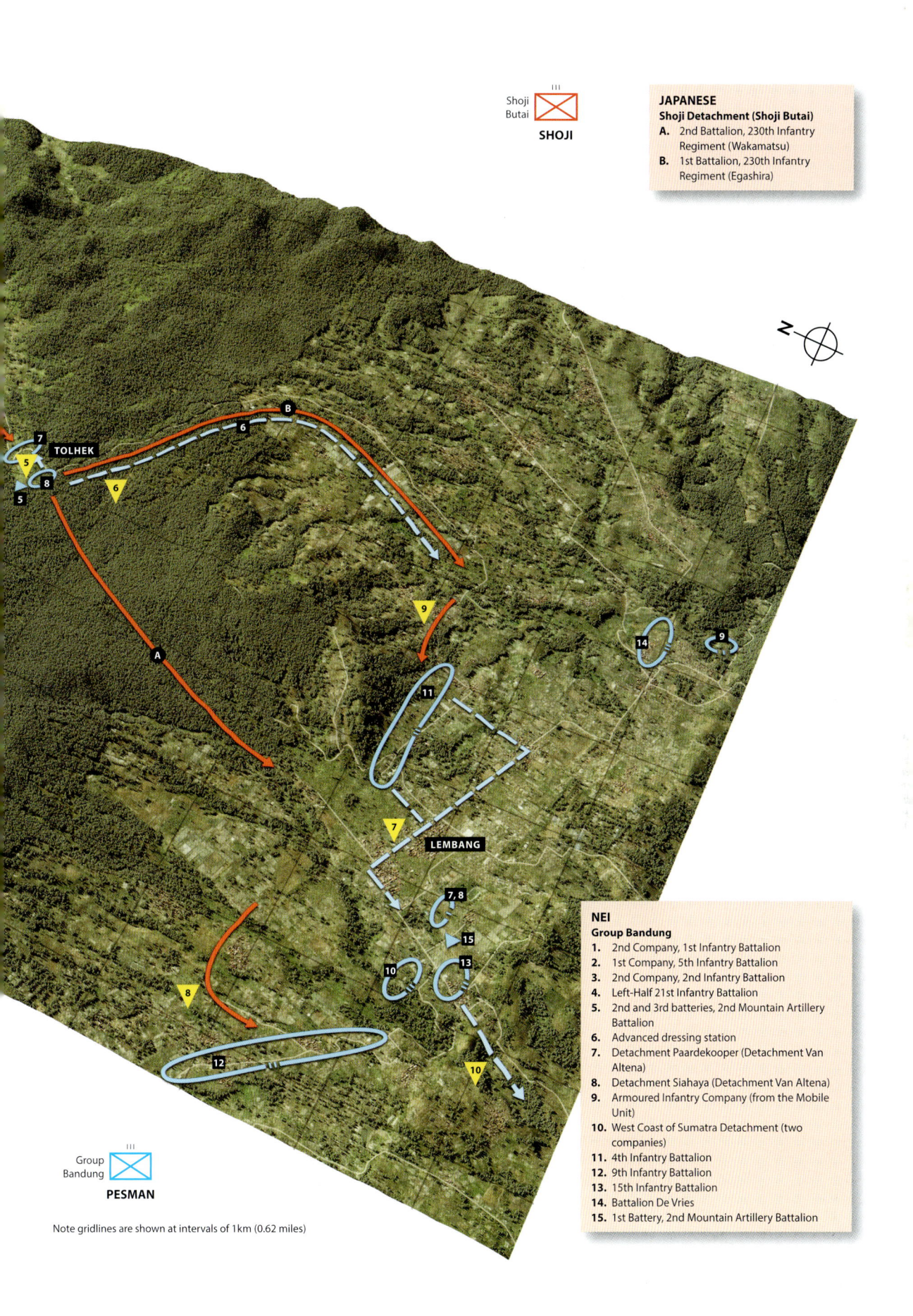

**JAPANESE**
**Shoji Detachment (Shoji Butai)**
A. 2nd Battalion, 230th Infantry Regiment (Wakamatsu)
B. 1st Battalion, 230th Infantry Regiment (Egashira)

SHOJI

TOLHEK

LEMBANG

Group Bandung

PESMAN

Note gridlines are shown at intervals of 1km (0.62 miles)

**NEI**
**Group Bandung**
1. 2nd Company, 1st Infantry Battalion
2. 1st Company, 5th Infantry Battalion
3. 2nd Company, 2nd Infantry Battalion
4. Left-Half 21st Infantry Battalion
5. 2nd and 3rd batteries, 2nd Mountain Artillery Battalion
6. Advanced dressing station
7. Detachment Paardekooper (Detachment Van Altena)
8. Detachment Siahaya (Detachment Van Altena)
9. Armoured Infantry Company (from the Mobile Unit)
10. West Coast of Sumatra Detachment (two companies)
11. 4th Infantry Battalion
12. 9th Infantry Battalion
13. 15th Infantry Battalion
14. Battalion De Vries
15. 1st Battery, 2nd Mountain Artillery Battalion

On 2 March 1942, Major-General Cox had to give up his best battalion, the Left-Half 21st Infantry Battalion, to Bandung Group.

The remaining units of the 2nd Division consisted of Home Guard, Town and Rural Guards and Veteran Reserve Corps elements with a low combat value. These were tasked with offering resistance on the outskirts of the built-up areas of Surakarta, Yogyakarta, Semarang and Magelang, without this developing into sustained fighting, and then surrendering. The aim was to slow the Japanese advance. The roads running from the north coast to the south coast had their bridges destroyed and were partly blocked with felled trees.

The Japanese advance progressed smoothly, and was only delayed by the state of the roads. No significant opposition was encountered from the NEI territorial troops. Sakaguchi sent his main force, the Yamamoto Echelon (HQ 146th Infantry Regiment and three companies) along with the Kanauji Echelon, from Yogyakarta along the coastal road directly towards Cilacap on 5 March 1942. He directed the Matsumoto Echelon (3rd Battalion, reduced) towards Magelang. At Surakarta and Magelang, a large number of NEI territorial troops were captured. The Kanauji Echelon reached the Serayu River on 6 March. However, all bridges had been destroyed.

South Group received reinforcements, but also lost men through desertion. One night, virtually an entire company of the Mangku Negoro Battalion deserted. In the evening of 7 March 1942, the Japanese crossed the river in the south. Group South offered little resistance and was ordered to withdraw. Cilacap was occupied in the morning of 8 March 1942. The fight for Central Java was over.

A number of roads were blocked by NEI troops using obstacles such as felled teak trees or crates packed with rubble, and bridges were destroyed. These barriers slowed the Japanese advance down significantly. The NEI territorial troops did not offer much resistance. In the last week of February 1942, Central Java was largely cleared of regular NEI troops. This motorized column of the Sakaguchi Detachment is shown on the march from Kragan; a Type 1 four-wheeled, 2.72-ton Toyota KB truck heads the column. (Mainichi Newspapers)

### East Java

The conquest of East Java was assigned to the IJA 48th Division. This motorized division was first deployed as part of the Fourteenth Army in the attack on the Philippines. After the capture of Manila, the formation was taken out of the line and prepared for shipment. Based on its experience in the Philippines, the 48th Division's leadership convinced Sixteenth Army to amend the operational plan for Java by reducing the number of landing points from two to one and concentrating on one objective: Surabaya. After the landings, Lieutenant-General Yuitsu Tsuchihashi, the commanding officer of 48th Division, wanted to quickly secure the crossing points over the Solo River and the oil installations at Cepu. Making the most of his mobility, he then planned a rapid advance from Cepu with his main force toward the Brandas River. He expected the decisive battle to take place there. After the defeat of the enemy forces, he would capture Porong and attack Surabaya from the south. A diversionary or fixing attack was planned along the Solo River. The division was organically equipped with sufficient motor vehicles to transport one-third of the infantry. In the Philippines, however, enough vehicles were seized to transport the entire division.

East Java and the island of Bali were part of the NEI 3rd Military Department under Major-General G.A. Ilgen, who also commanded the 3rd Division. This division, also known as the Surabaya Detachment, was tasked with defending Surabaya naval base. The static defence of the base was assigned to the Surabaya Security Force (*Veiligheidsbezetting Soerabaja*). The Mobile Group – consisting of 6th Infantry Regiment, 3rd Cavalry Squadron, 1st Field Artillery Battalion and the US Battery E, 2nd Battalion, 131st Field Artillery Regiment – was tasked with the mobile defence of the naval base. On 1 March 1942, the RNN Commander at Surabaya made some naval ground forces available to Ilgen. The Naval Battalion was formed, consisting of a HQ, four companies of marines and naval guards, a machine-gun section and logistics train, with a total strength of approximately 400 men.

After the destruction of the fleet, Surabaya had lost its significance as a naval base. As at Singapore, Major-General Ilgen and his troops were defending an empty base.

On 1 March 1942, the Japanese invasion fleet anchored at Kragan. Allied air raids sank one ship while a second ship was left stranded. A total of 62 personnel were killed and 210 wounded. However, these losses did not stop the landing going ahead at 0345 and 0400hrs. Rembang was quickly captured as a supply base. Despite roadblocks, the Solo River was reached in the afternoon of 2 March. The division found all the bridges and the Cepu Refinery destroyed, and the oil wells were on fire. The bridging of the swollen Solo River took more than a day. In the evening of 4 March, the Abe Unit (the main force) began to advance towards Kertosono on the Brandas River. As it advanced, the 48th Division received full air support.

Following the air strikes on the Japanese landing fleet at Kragan, FEAF ceased operations and evacuated equipment and personnel to Australia on 1 and 2 March 1942. The Java Air Command had not authorized this and lodged a protest. The Military Aviation Service also had to evacuate the airfields in Central and East Java for Andir.

Major-General Ilgen planned an offensive action by his Mobile Group on 28 February 1942 against the expected Japanese landing. However, he soon reneged on this decision. Instead, Ilgen decided to move to the defensive with

**ABOVE LEFT**
A Dutch Marine corporal of the Naval Battalion, March 1942. He wears the grey-green service dress, introduced in 1940. This was almost identical to the RNEI Army Model 1937 field dress. He poses with a Thompson sub-machine gun. More than three-quarters of the Naval Battalion's cadre was equipped with this firearm. (Netherlands Institute of Military History)

**ABOVE RIGHT**
The Tanaka Unit (two battalions of the 2nd Formosan Infantry Regiment and an artillery battalion) of the 48th Division comes ashore at Kragan (landing area No. 3) as the Second Echelon. The division was fully motorized with both organic and captured (on the Philippines) motor vehicles. A truck, probably a 2.88-ton Nissan 80, is hauled ashore manually. Some 700 locals were forced to help with the unloading. The Tanaka Unit's objective was Cepu, with its oil refinery and the bridges over the Solo River. (Collectie Stichting Nationaal Museum van Wereldculturen, Coll.nr. TM-10001990; CC BY-SA 4.0)

**RIGHT**
The NEI commanding officer in East Java was Major-General G.A. Ilgen, GOC of 3rd Division and 3rd Military Department. Ilgen was described as a very good divisional commander, an energetic and skilled leader, but prone to haste. During the campaign, his leadership lacked consistency. This, and his direct and detailed leadership style, led to confusion and ambiguity. Ilgen wears the uniform introduced shortly before the war with a grey-green short-sleeved shirt and shorts. (Nationaal Archief, public domain)

**FAR RIGHT**
When the bridges over the Solo River in East Java were destroyed, the IJA 48th Engineer Regiment and the attached 3rd Independent Engineer Regiment had to construct a temporary bridge to continue the advance towards the Brantas River. The bridge-building at Cepu was delayed because part of the new bridge was swept away by the swollen river. The next day, the repaired bridge was damaged once again, this time by the weight of an American M3 Stuart light tank captured in the Philippines. (Mainichi Newspapers)

the aim of gaining time for the destruction of the naval base. He wanted to fight a delaying action behind the Solo River to achieve this.

When the destruction in Surabaya was almost complete, on 4 March 1942 Ilgen's forces were freed up to conduct an offensive action. According to Ilgen, only forward-reconnaissance Japanese units at Ngawi and Bodjonegoro were active. Using his Mobile Group in a pincer move, he sought to recapture Cepu. Part of his mobile forces formed a blocking position behind the Brantas River. The plan of attack, based on an incorrect

A Japanese motorized column crossing the bridge over the Brandas River at Kediri. The bridge was seized intact. Leading the columns is an American half-track captured on the Philippines, followed by heavily camouflaged Nissan 80 trucks. Lieutenant-General Tsuchihashi, GOC of the 48th Division, had insisted more than once on the capture of the bridge at Kediri. However, his vanguard had focused on capturing the bridge at Kertosono and initially had not sent a unit to Kediri as planned. (Beeldbank WW2 – NIOD)

assessment of the enemy troops, could only end in failure. The troops lacked fire support and the southern pincer in particular was numerically too weak, not to mention the ambiguous nature of the orders issued. The northern axis of the NEI counter-attack clashed with the supporting attack of the Kitamura Unit (48th Reconnaissance Regiment) and was driven back. On the southern axis of advance, the De Iongh Detachment (3rd Cavalry Squadron and 10th Battalion, 6th Infantry Regiment) fought a delaying action against the vanguard of the Abe Unit and was driven back even before the Naval Battalion arrived. The Abe Unit reached Kertosono on 5 March 1942. The bridge over the Brantas was destroyed. Due to the rapid and powerful Japanese advance, the counter-attack ordered by Ilgen had come to an end before it had even started.

At Kertosono, the Japanese managed to force a passage over the Brandas the same day. The bridge at Kediri fell into Japanese hands undamaged that day. The blocking position behind the Brandas was thus compromised. The Abe Unit quickly advanced towards Porong. On 6 March 1942, the vanguard of the Abe Unit, comprising infantry supported by artillery, tanks and aircraft, launched an attack. The NEI defence was quickly broken and Porong occupied. Surabaya was thus surrounded. The 48th Division prepared to attack Surabaya on 9 March 1942. However, on 8 March, the white flag was raised. The battery from 17th Heavy Field Artillery, armed with 15cm howitzers and brought in especially from Manchuria for the attack on Surabaya, did not have to take action.

After the failure of the planned counter-attack, and the Japanese pincer movement towards Surabaya, Ilgen made preparations for the transition to guerrilla warfare. But the capitulation rendered this unnecessary. In the afternoon of 8 March 1942, the Japanese entered Surabaya.

A Dutch Naval Battalion LMG team, consisting of gunner and assistant. The weapon is a Breda M30 7.35mm LMG, captured from Italian troops in Africa and suplied by the British. (Collectie Mariniersmuseum, Rotterdam, 45789)

## SURRENDER

Against the background of a disintegrating RNEI Army and a crumbling NEI colonial administration, Major-General Pesman offered a local surrender in the evening of 7–8 March 1942. However, Lieutenant-General Imamura wanted to take the opportunity to enforce an overall capitulation. Negotiations took place on 8 March in Kalidjati between Imamura on the one hand, and Governor General Van Starkenborgh Stachouwer and Lieutenant-General Ter Poorten on the other. The NEI delegation had to accept the inevitable. Moreover, the Japanese were threatening to bomb Bandung. The RNEI Army capitulated on 9 March 1942.

The British, Australian and American troops in Java signed a capitulation agreement in Bandung on 12 March 1942. Brigadier Blackburn had wanted to continue the battle south of Bandung after the

This war painting by Koiso Ryohei shows the first meeting, in the evening of 8 March 1942 in an officers' house at Kalidjati Airfield, between the commanders of the Japanese Sixteenth Army and the RNEI Army. The Japanese delegation is seated to the right of the table, and the NEI military delegation to the left. (KTOMM Bronbeek)

capitulation of the RNEI Army in hopes of diverting to Australia. However, he could not make contact with Australia. Without supplies of food, ammunition and medicine, surrender would have just been a matter of time. He, too, thus accepted the inevitable.

Between 7 December 1941 and 8 March 1942, approximately 1,500 European and Indonesian soldiers of the RNEI Army were killed in action. Because the data of the Dutch War Graves Commission is incomplete, the true number is probably higher. The Royal Netherlands Navy suffered 1,650 casualties. Prisoner-of-war numbers are given in Table 11:

**Table 11: Allied POW numbers**

| Unit | Red Cross | Senshi Sosho[1] |
|---|---|---|
| RNEI Army, European | 38,400 | |
| Royal Netherlands Navy | 3,800 | |
| NEI forces | | 66,219 |
| British | 5,600 | 10,626 |
| Australians | 2,800 | 4,890 |
| Americans | 912 | 883 |

[1] The official military history of Imperial Japan's involvement in the Pacific War from 1937 to 1945.

On 9 March 1942, Lieutenant-General H. ter Poorten and Lieutenant-General Hitoshi Imamura met once again to finalize details and to sign the surrender agreement. Afterwards, a group photo was taken on the veranda of the house. In the middle is Lieutenant-General Hitoshi Imamura, with tropical helmet in hand, accompanied by staff members. To the left of him, in the back row, wearing spectacles is Major-General Saburo Endo. To the right of Imamura stands Major-General R. Bakkers, Lieutenant-General H. ter Poorten, Lieutenant-Colonel P.G. Mantel and (in the second row, behind Mantel) interpreter Captain J.D. Thijs. (Beeldbank WW2 – NIOD)

Figures are missing for Indonesian prisoners of war. Indonesian Muslim prisoners of war were released from April 1942 onwards. Christian Ambonese and Menadonese prisoners of war are excluded.

The losses for Japanese Sixteenth Army amounted to 311 killed and 832 wounded. Losses for the IJN's Netherlands East Indies Unit totalled 285 killed and 361 wounded.

# OPERATION *T* (NORTHERN SUMATRA)

After the conquest of Palembang and the advance to Bandar Lampung, the IJA 38th Division had also captured Bengkulu and Djambi respectively on 24 February and 4 March 1942. Central and North Sumatra were still in Dutch hands.

The NEI troops in North and Central Sumatra consisted of lightly armed garrison infantry supplemented with militia, Home Guard and Town Guards. Tactical units did not exceed one or more brigades of 20 men. Even before the Japanese attacked, armed resistance against Dutch colonial authority erupted in Aceh in February 1942. The RNEI Army troops in Aceh were then largely deployed to quell this, and after the Japanese landings also protected the evacuation of the European population and relatives of Indonesian soldiers.

On 12 March 1942, the IJA Imperial Guard Division landed in four locations on North and East Sumatra as planned. The landings were uncontested. The NEI units suffered from large-scale desertion among Indonesian soldiers. European troops maintained their cohesion, but lacked any fighting spirit. On 28 March 1942, the remaining NEI units capitulated.

# AFTERMATH

After the Java Campaign had ended, large parts of the Netherlands East Indies remained unoccupied. In three operations, New Guinea and the Lesser Sunda Islands were occupied without a fight between March and May. The islands located between New Guinea and Australia followed between late July and September 1942. In July, these islands were occupied by small NEI detachments from Australia (Operation *Plover*). Only Merauke in the far south of New Guinea remained in Dutch hands.

The IJA and IJN had driven the Western Powers from Asia and secured an immense area. In order to preserve these achievements, the second stage of operations would shift from the offensive to the defensive, securing the perimeter. Western counter-attacks would fail. The war would end in a compromise peace, whereby the Western Powers would have to accept the Japanese dominant position in South-East Asia. In the second stage, Japan would wage a war of attrition against the largest industrialized power, the United States. As the weaker party, Japan could not hope to win this battle of attrition. The intended limited war thus became total war, with the inevitable demise of the Japanese Empire.

During the Southern Offensive, the IJA and the IJN regularly clashed over the implementation and the timetable. Both parties fundamentally differed in operational terms. The IJA wanted to quickly occupy strategic points and wage battle so that the enemy did not have time to organize his defence. The IJN advocated a systematic approach consisting of an air campaign aimed at gaining air superiority by taking out enemy airpower at the landing site, but also in the hinterland. Only then could the amphibious landings take place. The IJN reported overly optimistic results from their air campaign. Partly as a result of this, their amphibious landings regularly faced Allied air strikes and attacks by naval units. Despite the previous air campaign, these turned out to be insufficiently disabled, if at all.

The Netherlands East Indies campaign took place in an extremely unfavourable period of the year: the wet monsoon. The Japanese air operations suffered from bad to very bad weather. It was not always possible to fly and provide air cover to the land and naval forces. In addition, heavy rainfall rendered airfields virtually unusable. The sodden airfields and runways that were too short had a negative impact on the effectiveness of the air branch. The Japanese had underestimated this point in their planning. On the other hand, Japanese ground troops regularly used rain and mist to surprise the NEI defenders.

The RNEI Army, in terms of operations, tactics and command, turned out to be qualitatively inferior to its Japanese opponent. The NEI was committed

Three of the four NEI static coastal batteries were located on the south-west coast of Tarakan. At Peningki these were two batteries each of 3 x 7.5cm L/40 guns and the Karoengan Battery of 4 x 12cm L/40 guns to guard the mine barriers in front of the Lingkas Front. The batteries are still partly intact including the guns. This picture dates from around 2010 and shows a rusty, rapid-fire 12cm L/40 No. 2 gun on a concrete foundation of Karoengan Battery. The gun had a cradle gun carriage on a pivot mounting with an armoured shield. It was a naval artillery piece made by Krupp in 1901. The gun was operated by a gun crew comprising gun commander and five gunners plus an assistant and ammunition carriers. (Private collection)

to a defensive struggle in an alliance. However, it had no influence over these allies. The interests with and between the Allies were not parallel ones. Great Britain and the United States were also too weak at this stage of the war to slow the Japanese advance, let alone stop it. A combined (multinational) headquarters was set up only a month after the outbreak of the war. This was too late. Operationally, the concept of indirect defence with horizontal bombers failed. The Military Aviation Service had too few bombing and combat aircraft to successfully implement it. Horizontal bombers were also rather unsuccessful against ships. The Japanese often achieved tactical surprise against the NEI defenders. On Ambon and Timor, they made amphibious landings on coasts that were considered unsuitable.

Tactically, the aggressive and mobile Japanese put the RNEI Army on the wrong track. Japanese air superiority was paralyzing to the NEI units. When aircraft approached, troops immediately sought cover and remained there for long periods of time. Against such an opponent, the NEI troops and in particular the Indonesian components showed insufficient willingness to fight. The RNEI Army faltered psychologically in terms of military capability. Combat intelligence was often lacking. As a result, the strength and direction of Japanese attacks were unknown. This made realistic counter-measures extremely difficult. The RNEI Army failed to demonstrate sufficient control when attacking. Planning and coordination were moderate to poor. As a result, counter-attacks took place in a fragmented manner and with forces that were too weak. In the counter-attack of the 2nd Infantry Regiment and Teerink Group, the advance to contact was started according to the rules, i.e. when the attackers were within range of their artillery – c. 15km. As a result, troops jumped off kilometres ahead of the attack target and had to advance in battle formation for hours through tough terrain under tropical temperatures. The result was the loss of the element of surprise and exhaustion among the attacking troops – and all this in the face of enemy air superiority. Artillery was deployed in a hesitant and fragmented manner. Australian Major J.H. Brown had pointed out the shortcomings in an exercise in November 1941: 'No coordinated fire plan had been prepared nor had any recce been made by battalion commanders … Three hours after daylight the two attacking battalions had moved forward about a mile and still well behind the front line were having breakfast. The impression was that the attack suffered from lack of drive from above and would have been fatal in practice.' Brown saw the main weakness 'in the battalion and regimental commanders who lack practical experience'. Based on his findings, the Australian Director of Military Intelligence stated that 'the army is well equipped. Their training is mainly defensive and their knowledge of offensive tactics is more theoretical than practical.'[15]

Command was sometimes chaotic. Division commanders had direct contact with company-level commanders and vice versa, bypassing the hierarchical command lines.

With the conquest of the Netherlands East Indies, Japan had seized coveted petroleum production and refining capacity and other strategic raw materials. Limiting ourselves to petroleum, the wells and installations in the Netherlands East Indies had been largely destroyed. These demolitions were aimed at preventing their use for six months. The Japanese managed

---

15  AWM 54, 431/13/17, N.E.I. Defence Forces.

to restart extraction and refining relatively quickly, although pre-war production figures were not achieved. Palembang accounted for 78 per cent of Japan's aviation fuel consumption and 22 per cent of crude oil.

**Table 12: Petroleum production in the NEI**

| Period | Production in million tons | Production in million barrels | Export to Japan in per cent |
|---|---|---|---|
| April 1942 to March 1943 | 4 | 29 | 40 |
| April 1943 to March 1944 | 7 | 51 | 30 |
| April 1944 to March 1945 | 5.5 | 40 | 14 |
| April 1945 to Japanese surrender | 1 | 7 | 0 |

The transport of extracted and refined petroleum to Japan turned out to be a bottleneck. Japan lacked a tanker fleet with sufficient capacity. In 1939, the Japanese tanker fleet comprised 38 ships with a total capacity of 3,124 million barrels. That was less than 10 per cent of annual imports. Oil imports were largely transported by ships from other countries, ones with which Japan came into conflict. This presented the country with an almost unsolvable problem.

The US submarine offensive and aircraft attacks played havoc among the Japanese tanker fleet. 'Japan ended up continuing the war, again suffering from an extreme shortage of fuel'.[16]

Alongside the defeat by Japan, the Netherlands East Indies also disintegrated on 8 March 1942. Three years of heavy occupation followed. European influence in the Netherlands East Indies was almost completely nullified. The prisoners of war were partly employed outside Java for the construction of airfields on, for example, the island of Flores and railway lines in Burma–Siam or on Sumatra and in mines in Japan. Of the 42,233 European prisoners of war taken, 8,200 (19.4 per cent) died. The European population was partly interned in civilian camps. This involved an estimated 100,000 persons. Of these, 16,800 died. About 120,000 Europeans remained outside the camps.

The Japanese, greeted as liberators, inflicted a heavy toll on Indonesia. Hunger is said to have killed 2.5 million Indonesians. Japan employed a large number of mainly Javanese as workers. Some of these *romusha* (forced labourers) were employed on a temporary basis. It is estimated that between 160,000 and 200,000 were deployed outside Java. Many died in the process.

The Japanese occupation served as a multiplier for the Indonesian independence movement. The occupation policy was not aimed at granting independence within the Greater East Asian Co-Prosperity Sphere. Indonesia had to be made serviceable to the Japanese war effort. Japan gradually changed its attitude as the war changed course. In September 1944, Japan declared that it would grant Indonesia independence in the near future. In August 1945, it went a step further and promised independence. However, on 15 August 1945, Japan was forced to surrender, negating further cooperation over Indonesian independence.

Two days after the Japanese capitulation, the Indonesian leaders Mohammad Hatta and Sukarno took the initiative, declaring Indonesian independence on 17 August 1945. It would take four more years of negotiation and warfare before the Netherlands recognized this.

16 Remmelink, *The Operations of the Navy* (2018), p. 589.

# FURTHER READING

**Primary records**
Museum Bronbeek, 2012/11/26-4-1, Bakkers, R., *Het Koninklijk Nederlands-Indische Leger voor en gedurende zijn strijd tegen de Japanse invasie*, typoscript z.p., z.j. [1947]
Nationaal Archief, Den Haag, Meyer Ranneft, 2.21.121, inv. nr. 477, Poorten, H. ter, Verslag omtrent mijn beleid als legercommandant, Geheim – Eigenhandig, 30 januari 1946
Nederlands Instituut voor Militaire Historie, Den Haag, Nederlands-Indië contra Japan (1940–1946), Toegang 508

**Secondary sources**
Boer, P.C., *De luchtstrijd rond Borneo: Operaties van de Militaire Luchtvaart KNIL in de periode december 1941 tot februari 1942*, Van Holkema & Warendorf, Houten 1987
——, *De luchtstrijd om Indië: Operaties van de Militaire Luchtvaart KNIL in de periode december 1941 tot maart 1942*, Van Holkema & Warendorf, Houten 1990
——, *Het verlies van Java: Een kwestie van Air Power: De eindstrijd om Nederlands-Indië van de geallieerden lucht-, zee- en landstrijdkrachten in de periode van 18 februari t/m 7 maart 1942*, De Bataafsche Leeuw, Amsterdam 2006 (available in English as: Boer, P.C., *The Loss of Java: The Final Battles for the Possession of Java Fought by Allied Air, Naval and Land Forces in the Period of 18 February–7 March 1942*, Singapore University Press, Singapore, 2011)
Boester, A.J.Th. e.a., *Nederlands-Indië contra Japan*, Staatsdrukkerij- en uitgeversbedrijf Bandoeng/'s-Gravenhage 1949–1961, 7 delen
Bussemaker, H.Th., *Paradise in Peril: Western Colonial Power and Japanese Expansion in South-East Asia, 1905–1941*, Thesis, Universiteit van Amsterdam, 2001. Available at: http://dare.uva.nl/document/100764
Donovan, Patrick H., *Oil Logistics in the Pacific War: In and After Pearl Harbor*, Air Command and Staff College Air University, Maxwell AFB, 2001
Francillon, R.J., *Japanese Aircraft of the Pacific War*, Putnam & Company, London, 1970
Kiyoshi Aizawa, 'Japanese Strategy in the First Phase of the Pacific War'. Available at: www.nids.mod.go.jp/english/event/forum/pdf/2009/04.pdf
Lohnstein, Marc, *Netherlands East Indies Army 1936–1942*, Osprey Publishing Ltd., Oxford, 2018
*Reports of General MacArthur: Japanese Operations in the Southwest Pacific Area Volume II – Part I*. Available at: https://history.army.mil/books/wwii/MacArthur Reports/MacArthur V2 P1/macarthurv2.htm
Minoru Nomura, 'The Dutch East Indies and the Japanese Armed Forces', Military History Department, National Defence College, Tokyo, Japan, March 4, 2010
Nortier, J.J., 'Orde- en rustverstoring in het Djambische februari 1942', *Militaire Spectator*, 152, 1983, pp. 565–77
——, 'De gevechten bij Palembang in februari 1942', *Militaire Spectator*, 154, 1985, 7, pp. 312–25
——, 'De gevechten bij Palembang in februari 1942, Deel 2', *Militaire Spectator*, 154, 1985, 8, pp. 355–68
——, 'De gevechten in Atjeh van maart 1942', *Stabelan*, 12, 1986, 3, pp. 11–17
——, 'De gevechten in Atjeh van maart 1942, Deel II', *Stabelan*, 12, 1986, 4, pp. 40–48
——, *De Japanse aanval op Nederlands-Indië*, Uitgeversmaatschappij Ad. Donker, Rotterdam, 1988
——, *De Japanse aanval op Nederlands-Indië, Deel 2 Borneo*, Uitgeversmaatschappij Ad. Donker, Rotterdam, 1992
——, 'De gevechten van het Commando Midden-Sumatra, februari/maart 1942', *Stabelan*, 20, 1994, 3, pp. 2–12
——, 'De gevechten van het Commando Midden-Sumatra, februari/maart 1942, Deel 2', *Stabelan*, 20, 1994, 4, pp. 2–12
——, 'De gevechten van het Commando Midden-Sumatra, februari/maart 1942, slot', *Stabelan*, 21, 1994, 1, pp. 2–10
——, Kruijt, P. and Groen, P.M.H., *De Japanse aanval op Java: Maart 1942*, De Bataafsche Leeuw, Amsterdam, 1994
Record, Jeffrey, 'Japan's Decision for War in 1941: Some Enduring Lessons', Strategic Studies Institute, February 2009. Available at: https://www.hsdl.org/?view&did=38470
Remmelink, Willem (ed. and trans.), *The Invasion of the Dutch East Indies*, The Corts Foundation/Leiden University Press, 2015
——, *The Operations of the Navy in the Dutch East Indies and the Bay of Bengal*, The Corts Foundation/Leiden University Press, 2018
Stille, Mark, *Java Sea 1942: Japan's Conquest of the Netherlands East Indies*, Osprey Publishing Ltd., Oxford, 2019
Willmott, H.P., *Empires in the Balance: Japanese and Allied Pacific Strategies to April 1942*, Orbis Publishing, London, 1982
Womack, Tom, *The Allied Defence of the Malay Barrier 1941–1942*, McFarland and Company, Jefferson, 2016

# INDEX

Page numbers in **bold** refer to illustrations and numbers in brackets are caption locators.

ABDACOM  12, 13, 33–35, **34**, 45, 49, 59, 64, 65, 66
air attacks  40, **41**, 45, 49, 57, 59, 63, 65, 71–72, 75, **77**, **83**, 87
aircraft  19, **38**, 57, **63**
airfields  17–18, 31–32, 37–38, **38**, **41**, 45, 48, **48**, 54
　defence of  50, **50**
　Kalidjati Airfield  74–75, **74**, 76
Allied forces
　armament  22
　Australian  21–22
　British  22, 48
　commanders  12–15, **13**, **14**, **15**
　operational plans  33–35
　United States (US)  22
　*see also* RNEI Army; Royal Netherlands Navy
Ambon  48–50, **50**, **52–53**
amphibious operations  17, 40, 51, 63, 64, **64**, 66, 67, 72–73, **72**, 74, 87, **87**
armoured vehicles  **19**, **20**, **39**, 66, **78–79** (80), **88**
artillery  50, 56, 58, 92
Australian forces  22, 35, 49, 50, 56, 64, 65, 66, 68–69, 76, **76**

Bakkers, Maj.-Gen. Rudolph  12, 13, **32**, 90
Bali  65
Balikpapan  12, 29, 32, 40–41, 45, **45**
Bandjermasin  51, 54
Berryman, Brig. F.H.  56
bicycles  81
Blackburn, Brig. Arthur Seaforth  15, **15**, 22, 76, **76**, 89–90
Blackforce  22, 76, **76**, 81
Borneo  37
bridge building  **88**
Brown, Maj. J.H.  92

Cam Ranh Agreement 1942  38, 51
campaign events
　aftermath  91–93
　Ambon  48–50, **50**, **52–53**
　Bali  65
　Balikpapan  40–41, 45, **45**
　Bandjermasin  51, 54
　chronology  8–9
　Java  69–89, **70** (71), **72**, 73, 74, 75, 76, 77, **78–79** (80), **81**, **82**, **83**, **84–85**, **86**, **87**, **88**, **89**
　Kendari  45
　Makassar  51
　Menado  39–40, **40**, **41**, **46–47**
　Palembang  54–65, **55**, 56, 57, 59, 60–61 (62)
　Phase I operations  37–38

Phase II operations, conquest of the NEI  38–39
Phase III operations  45
Singkawang  45, 48
surrender of RNEI Army  89–90, **89**, **90**
Tarakan  39, **39**, **42–43** (44)
Timor  65–69
campaign origins  5–7
　Japanese expansion  5, 7
　oil, Japanese need of  6
casualties and losses  39, 40, 45, 48, 50, 51, 59, 68, 69, 80, 87, 90
Churchill, Winston  33–34
civilians  12, 18, 41, 93
coastal batteries  **92**
commanders
　Allied  12–15, **13**, **14**, **15**, 92
　Japanese  10–12, **10**, **11**, **12**
Cox, Maj.-Gen. P.A.  83, 86

desertions  51, 65, 86, 90
disease  22, 49, 54, 68

Endo, Maj.-Gen. Saburo  11, **11**, 81, 90

flags  **64**

Great Britain  29, 31, 33, 92
Greater East Asian Co-Prosperity Sphere  5, 6
guerrilla warfare  32, 33

Hoogenband, Lt.-Col. C. Van den  41
Hunter, Air Cdre Henry J.F.  56, 59, 64

Ilgen, Maj.-Gen. G.A.  87–88, **88**, 89
Imamura, Lt.-Gen. Hitoshi  10, **10**, 73, 76, 89, 90
Imperial General Headquarters (IGHQ)  16
Imperial Japanese Army (IJA)  41, 51, 57, 71
　armament  20
　bicycles, use of  81
　clashes with IJN  91
　command and control problems  73
　counter-clockwise advance plan  27, 28
　effectiveness  17
　orders of battle  23
　strength  20, 73
　structure  16
　training  16
Imperial Japanese Army (IJA), units
　Sixteenth Army  16, 69, 72, 73, 77, 86, 90
　Southern Army  **26**, 27–28, 38, 48, 57, 69, 77
　2nd Div  16, 72, 77, **81**
　38th Div  16, 49–50, 57, 64, 90
　48th Div  16, 72, 86, 87, 89
　1st Formosan Infantry Rgt  65
　2nd Raiding Rgt  57, 58–59, **60–61**

　(62), 63, 64, **64**
　2nd Reconnaissance Rgt  73–74
　16th Infantry Rgt  76
　146th Infantry Rgt  **42–43** (44)
　228th Infantry Rgt  49–50, 67, 68, 69
　229th Infantry Rgt  57, 63
　230th Infantry Rgt  10, 11
　1st Raiding Group  16, 57
　56th Mixed Infantry Group  16
　Fukushima Detachment  74, 77, 81
　Ito Detachment  49–50, 66, 67, 68, 69
　Kawaguchi Detachment  37, 48
　Nasu Detachment  73, 76, 77
　Sakaguchi Detachment  11, 16, 17, 39, 40, 41, **42–43** (44), 45, 54, 72, 73, 83, 86
　Sato Detachment  74, 81
　Shoji Detachment  72, 74, 75, 77, **78–79** (80)
　Wakamatsu Raiding Unit  74, 81, 82
Imperial Japanese Navy (IJN)  16, 40–41, 45, 49, 54, 57–58, 63, 71, 90
　attacks on  45, 59, 63, 73, 87
　clashes with IJA  91
　clockwise advance plan  27, 28, 54
　Combined Fleet  17, 27, 67
　operational performance  17, 18
　orders of battle  24
　Southern Task Force  17, 49, 67, 69, 71
　Special Landing Forces (SLFs)  17, **17**, 40, **40**, **41**, **42–43** (44), 50, 51, 67–68, **67**
Indian Army  48
intelligence  28, 34, 73, 92
Ito, Maj.-Gen. Takeo  50
Iwakuni Agreement  **26**, 27–28

Japan  **36** (37)
　commanders  10–12, **10**, **11**, **12**
　expansion of  5, 7
　oil, need of  6, 92–93
　operational plans  27–28, 66
　orders of battle  23–24
　Southern Offensive  5, 10, 11, 16, 17, 28, **36** (37), 37
　US embargoes  7
Java  17, 18, 27, 29, 31, 45, 48, 54
　air offensive against  71–72
　amphibious operations  72–73, **72**, 74, 87, **87**
　central Java  83, 86, **86**
　Ciater Pass  81–83, **82**, **84–85**
　command lines and troop positions  71
　defence of  32–33, 35
　East Java  86–89, **87**, **88**, **89**
　invasion of  69–89, **70**(71), 73
　Subang  75–76, 77, **78–79**(80)
　surrender of RNEI Army  89–90, **89**, **90**
　troop strengths  73
　West Java  73–83, **73**, **74**, 75, 76, 77, **78–79** (80), **81**, 83
Java Sea, Battle of  72

Kapitz, Lt.-Col. J.L.R. 49
Kendari 40, 45

Lavarack, Lt.-Gen. J.D. 56, 57
Leggatt, Lt.-Col. W.W. 66, 67, 68

Maguire, Wg Cdr H.G. 58
Makassar 51
Mantel, Lt.-Col. P.G. **32**, 90
Marshall, Gen. George C. 34
Menado 39–40, **40**, **41**, 46–47
Military Aviation Service 14–15, 19, 31, 33, 37, 39, 40, 45, 49, 63, 75, 87, 92
morale 48, 68, 76, 83

Nasu, Maj.-Gen. Yumio 76
Netherlands 33, 35, 37, 38
Netherlands East Indies (NEI)
  independence 93
  map **4**
  military staff conferences 6
  neutrality 29
  oil production 6
  operational doctrine 31
  operational plans 29–33, **30**
  orders of battle 24–25
  political situation **20**
  rubber production 6
New Principles of Defence (NEI) 1927 29, 31

Ohl, Capt. J.H.M.U.L.E. 60–61 (62)
Oijen, Maj.-Gen Ludolph Hendrik van 14–15, **15**, 69
oil production 5, 7, 54
  after Japanese invasion 93
  defence of refineries 58–59, **59**, 60–61 (62)
  destruction of infrastructure 39, **39**, 41, 45, 63, 92
  fuel for ships, planes and war 6
Operation *A-Go see* Japan, Southern Offensive
Operation *B* 37
Operation *H* 28, 37, 38–39, 69–89, 70 (71)
Operation *L* 54–65, **55**, **56**, **57**, **59**, 60–61 (62)
Operation *T* 90
Operation *Z* 71
operational plans
  Allies 33–35
  codenames 28
  Japanese 27–28, 66
  maps **26**, **30**, **36** (37)
  Netherlands East Indies 29–33, **30**
  staff conferences 1940–41 33
  unified command (ABDACOM) 1942 33–35, **34**
*Orcades*, HMT 64, **65**
orders of battle
  Japanese 23–24
  Netherlands East Indies 24–25
Ozawa, V. Adm. Jisaburo 57–58, 63

paintings 57, 77, 83, 89
Palembang 54–65, **55**, **56**, **57**, **59**, 60–61 (62), 93
paratroopers 40, **40**, **41**, **41**, 58, **58**, 59, 60–61 (62), 64, 67–68, **67**
Pesman, Maj.-Gen. Jacob Jan 14, **14**, 75, 89
pillboxes 32, 42–43 (44), 50, 81, **82**
Plans for the Employment of Naval and Air Forces 21
Poorten, Lt.-Gen. Hein Ter 12–13, **13**, 14, 35, **35**, 69, **90**
prisoners of war 18, **18**, 39, 40, 41, 48, 50, 63, 68, 82, 90, 93

reconnaissance 45, 49, 75, 76
RNEI Army 18–21, 29, 37, 40, 45, 49–50, 74, 77, 90
  armament 20
  cavalry **19**
  command structure 18–19, 92
  desertions 51, 65, 86, 90
  effectiveness 91–92
  modernization 19–20
  orders of battle 24–25
  recruitment 18
  reinforcement 19
  strength 20, 73
  surrender in Java 89–90, **89**, **90**
RNEI Army units 67
  Bandung Group 14, 71, 77, **84–85**, 86
  South Group 83, 86
  2nd Div. 83, 86
  2nd Infantry Rgt 76, 77, 92
  4th Infantry Rgt 81–82, 83
  2nd Bn 48
  6th Infantry Bn 41
  10th Infantry Bn 56, 59, **59**, 60–61 (62), 63, 64, 65
  2nd Moluccas Garrison Bn 48–49, 50
  Celebes and Menado Garrison Bn 51
  Naval Bn 87, **87**, 89
  Palembang and Djambi Garrison Bn 56
  South-Eastern Borneo Garrison Bn 54
  Timor and Dependencies Garrison Bn 66
  West Borneo Garrison Bn 48
  Coastal and AA Artillery Co 41
  4th Coastal and AA Artillery Co 48
  Detachment Q 68–69
  Kupang Detachment 67
  Mobile Unit 75, **78–79**(80), 88–89
  motorized AT and AA companies 66
  Surabaya Detachment 87
roadblocks 58, 59, 68, 74, 86, **86**, 87
Roosevelt, Franklin D. 33–34
Royal Air Force (RAF) 22, 56, 57, 59, 64, 75
Royal Australian Air Force (RAAF) 21, 22, 40, 66, 75
Royal Navy 22
Royal Netherlands Navy 19, 29, 31, 33, 37, 48, 49, 90
  Naval Aviation Service 20, 38
  Netherlands East Indies Unit 51
  orders of battle 25
  strength 19–20

rubber 6
Ryohei, Koiso (artist) **89**

Sakaguchi, Maj.-Gen. Shizuo 11–12, **12**, 41, 83, 86
Schilling, Maj.-Gen. Wijbrandus 13–14, **14**, 74
Scott, Lt.-Col. W.J.R. 49, 50
Shoji, Maj.-Gen. Toshishige 1, 10–11, **11**, 77, 81
Singapore 27, 35, 64
Singkawang 45, 48
Stachouwer, Tjarda van Stakenborgh 12–13, 89
Stark, Harold R. 20
Steele, Brig. C.S. 59, 64
Straten, Lt.-Col. N.L.W. van 68, 69
Sumatra 90

tanks 20, 56, 73, 75
Tarakan 7, 29, 32, 39
  attack on NEI strongpoint No. 10, 11 January 1942 39, 42–43 (44)
Teerink, Maj. 75–76, 76–77
Terbrugge, Sgt. 42–43(44)
Third Air Force (Japan) 11, 23, 63, 71
Timor 65–69
Tokyo Agreement 1941 27
Tripartite Pact 1940 6
Tsuchihashi, Lt.-Gen. Yuitsu 86
Tsuruta, Goro (artist) **57**

uniforms 22, 59, 67, 87
United States (US) 31, 33, 92
  and Japan 5, 6, 7
  Two-Ocean Navy Act 1940 7
United States (US) Navy 28, 45, 71, 72
USAAF Far East Air Force (FEAF) 22, 40, 45, 63, 72, 87

Veale, Brig. W.C.D. 66, 67
Veen, Lt.-Col. W.P. van **32**
Veer, Col. W.J. 81–82, 82
Vogelesang, Lt.-Col. L.N.W. 56, 59, 63
Vooren, Col. M. 51
Vries, Maj. B.P. de 63

Waal, Lt.-Col. S. de 39, 42–43 (44)
Wakamatsu, Maj. 74, 81, 82
war crimes 10, 11, 18, **18**, 39, 40, 41, 50, 82
Wavell, Gen. Archibald P. 34, 35, **35**, 40, 56, 69
weaponry 20, 22, 58, **59**
  anti-tank rifles 38
  grenades 60–61 (62)
  machine guns 20, 32, 41, 66, 89
  sub-machine guns 87
weather 37, 91
Willmott, H.P. 31
Wulfhorst, Capt. G.J. 75–76

Yamamoto, Adm. Isoroku 67
Yoshioka, Kenji (artist) **77**